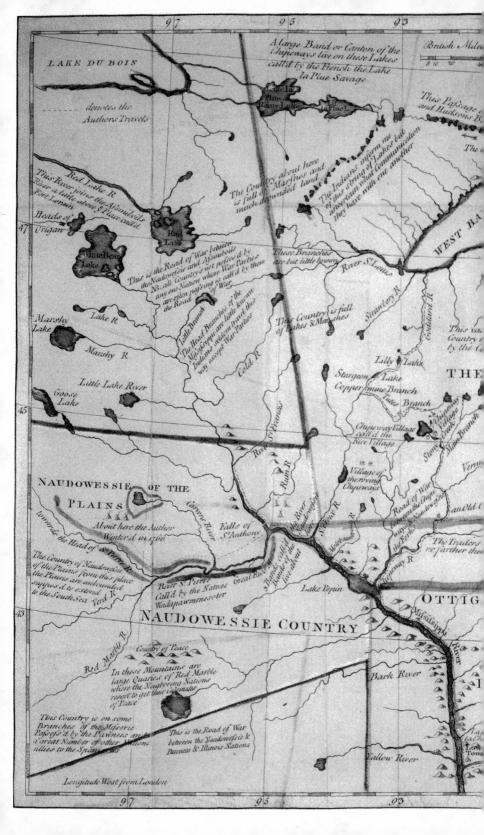

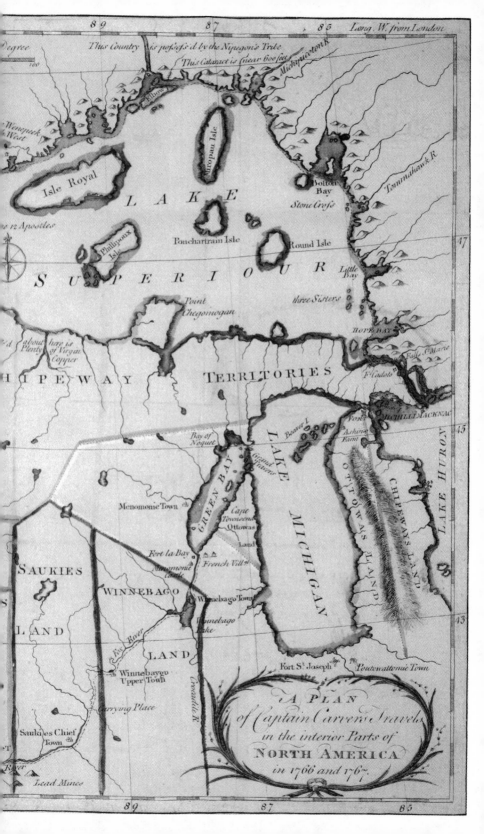

Jonathan Carver's

Travels Through America

1766–1768

Jonathan Carver's
Travels Through America
1766–1768

An Eighteenth-Century
EXPLORER'S ACCOUNT
of Uncharted America

EDITED *and with*
AN INTRODUCTION
by Norman Gelb

John Wiley & Sons, Inc.
New York • Chichester • Brisbane • Toronto • Singapore

ILLUST.

The copper engravings are from the original 1788 edition of Jonathan Carver's *Travels Through the Interior Parts of North America,* and were supplied courtesy of the New York Public Library.

In recognition of the importance of preserving what has been written, it is a policy of John Wiley & Sons, Inc., to have books of enduring value printed on acid-free paper, and we exert our best efforts to that end.

Copyright © 1993 by Norman Gelb
Published by John Wiley & Sons, Inc.

Library of Congress Cataloging-in-Publication Data

Jonathan Carver's travels through America, 1766–1768 : an eighteenth
-century explorer's account of uncharted America / edited and with
an introduction by Norman Gelb.
    p. cm.
    Includes bibliographical references and index.
    ISBN 0-471-57579-8 (cloth)
    1. Northwestern States—Description and travel. 2. Mississippi
River Valley—Description and travel. 3. Indians of North America—
Northwestern States—History—18th century. 4. Indians of North
America—Mississippi River Valley—History—18th century. 5. North
America—Discovery and exploration—English. 6. Carver, Jonathan,
1710–1780—Diaries. I. Gelb, Norman.
F597.J6 1993
917.704'1—dc20   92-19002

Printed in the United States of America

10 9 8 7 6 5 4 3 2 1

CONTENTS

CONTENTS

INTRODUCTION

The Life and Times
of Jonathan Carver

Jonathan Carver was born in Weymouth, Massachusetts, on April
13, 1710, at a time when the nation that was to become the United
States was no more than a cluster of British colonies hugging the
Atlantic coast of North America. Carver died in England seventy
years later, largely unknown but about to gain acclaim for the published account of his experiences while exploring part of the mostly
uncharted American hinterland.

With its detailed description of the New World's wilderness, and
particularly of the Indians Carver met, his book attracted wide and
favorable attention. It went through many editions, both in England,
where it was first published in 1778, and then in the fledgling United
States. It was also translated, fully or in abridged versions, into
Dutch, French, German, Swedish, and Greek. No writer had previously provided so comprehensive, intelligent, and well received an
account of America's backcountry. Carver's *Travels* was the first
genuinely popular American travel book.

The information it contained was used by later explorers and

I

authors for their own explorations or for literary research. Its description of the sprawling richness of the land and the glory of its landscape made a profound impression. But the greatest significance of the book was its picture of the native Americans Carver met and resided among. His portrayal of the way they lived, the beliefs they held, and their human qualities did much to alter the prevailing eighteenth-century image of Indians as "savages," although that label—signifying the denial of the benefits of civilization rather than implying a brutally barbaric nature—continued to be long used through habit, even by European settlers and American colonists who knew better.

Despite the high regard in which Carver's book was held at the end of the eighteenth and early in the nineteenth centuries, it subsequently lapsed into obscurity, becoming a curiosity, sought out only by those who knew to look for it. Nevertheless, it remains one of the earliest popular works of Americana, the product of an adventurous, resourceful, imaginative figure who looked into the remote wilds of his native land and recorded for posterity the pristine wonders of what he saw there.

The British and French Struggle for a Supremacy in North America

When Jonathan Carver was born, the vast American hinterland beyond the Appalachian Mountains was a mysterious region to most people living in the British colonies on the eastern seaboard. They heard stories about hostile Indians living there, and about exotic wildlife. They heard about plunging rivers, vast lakes, and towering mountains. But this information was mostly patchy, often exaggerated hearsay, circulated by itinerant traders and trappers or by some of the comparative few who lived on what was then the frontier.

The colonies had been in existence for less than a century. During most of that time, the colonists had devoted themselves to making the coastal plain their home. They had struggled for sustenance, security, and permanence. The growing influx of European immigrants was continuing and the settlement of land, although still confined to the area east of the Appalachian range, was expanding inexorably. A handful of cities—Philadelphia, Boston, New York, Charleston—were thriving. With the flood of slaves from Africa, plantations in the South were flourishing. But life on the frontier remained a struggle. It was subject to relentless uncertainties and dangers, among which were numbered the French and what they might be up to.

A rivalry between Great Britain and France for dominance in Europe had earlier spilled over into North America. The French had claimed colonial possession of a wide expanse of the North American continent. In addition to parts of southeastern Canada, this region included all the territory between the Appalachian range and the Mississippi River as well as much land even farther west. In Paris, France's stake in the New World was seen to have crucial symbolic significance. According to one of Louis XV's ministers, "It is possessions in America that will in the future form the balance of power in Europe" and if the English should prove dominant there, it "will usurp the commerce of the nations" and "she alone will remain rich in Europe."

During the French and Indian Wars—the European contest for supremacy in the New World—the Spanish were allied with the French. Spain claimed land in the American Southwest as well as Florida, but it played a comparatively minor role in the struggle. The French, however, were strategically positioned for the protracted conflict that began in 1689 and continued intermittently over a period of some seventy years.

The French had established a string of forts, fur trading posts, and communities clear across the American heartland—at Fort Niagara, Detroit, Fort Duquesne (Pittsburgh), Kaskaskia in present-day Illinois, Vincennes in Indiana, St. Louis, Fort Rosalie (Natchez), and New Orleans. These outposts had been hacked out of the wilderness not only to establish a French presence; they were the vanguard of what France hoped to fashion into a permanent North American presence. It would straddle the American heartland and, in time, if circumstances allowed, it was to dominate if not incorporate the colonies on the Atlantic coast.

To the inhabitants of the British colonies, the possibility of French success was frightening. There were communities of German, Irish, Dutch, Swedish, and other European settlers in the colonies, including French Huguenots who had fled there to escape religious persecution in their homeland. There were also great numbers of black slaves. But most of the colonists were of English ancestry, many having themselves arrived in the New World from Great Britain only a few years before.

While the French sought dominance in North America, many of the British American colonists looked longingly westward to the possibility of great rewards beyond the Appalachians. For them, the French were not merely an obstruction; nor were they only a physical threat to settlers on the frontier. For many of the colonists, the French menace took the form also of a foreign culture, a strange language, and a genuinely tyrannical monarchy, in contrast to the more enlightened British Crown.

There was also the question of French Catholicism, a religion commonly abhorred by the predominantly Protestant population of the British colonies, and the fact that the French military command had established working alliances with Indian tribes, some of which were prone to fearsome assaults on British American frontier settlements. Tales of such attacks, sometimes exaggerated but often not, spread terror in those areas. After an attack on the sparsely settled Schenectady, New York, a local man wrote, "The cruelties committed at said Place, no Penn can write nor Tongue expresse: the women bigg with Childe rip'd up and the Children alive throwne into the flames, and there heads dash'd in pieces against the Doors and windows."

To many, a succession of British setbacks indicated that a French victory in the contest for control was a genuine possibility. Those reversals included the surrender of young Colonel George Washington and his Virginia militia troops in 1754 to the French at Fort Necessity in the wilds of western Pennsylvania, near present-day Uniontown. Reverend Jonathan Edwards, the prominent Massachusetts theologian, preached the gospel against the French, fearing that

4

they would soon gain supremacy in North America. "God indeed is remarkably frowning on us," he intoned. "Our enemies get up above us very high, and we are brought down very low. . . . What will become of us God only knows."

But such forebodings were groundless. French defeat at the hands of the British and their American auxiliaries was inevitable. If nothing else, geopolitical factors would decide the issue.

By 1756 and the start of the Seven Years War, the last of the series of French and Indian Wars, the British colonies still occupied only a comparatively thin strip of coastal land, but they had been firmly established. Their inhabitants numbered some 1.5 million. Although the French claimed a far greater expanse of territory, they were far less numerous, with no more than about sixty thousand, a fraction of the British colonies' population. They were concentrated largely in southeastern Canada and New Orleans. Aside from soldiers at the various forts, in the regions north of the Mississippi Delta and between the Appalachians and the Mississippi, there may have been as few as two or three thousand French, virtually all men and mostly itinerant traders—hardly enough to contest the British colonists for dominance of the continent. Were it not for their alliance with various Indian tribes, the challenge the French presented would initially have appeared as futile as it ultimately became.

The struggle for North America between the two European empires effectively ended with the fall of Montreal to British and British American forces in 1760, although it was not officially concluded until the Treaty of Paris, sometimes called the Treaty of Versailles, was signed in 1763. In that treaty, the French surrendered to the British the territory to which they had laid claim between the Appalachians and the Mississippi, as well as in Canada. Spain also conceded defeat and surrendered Florida to the British. By agreement with the French, the Spanish now claimed possession of most of the territory west of the Mississippi. This land was too far away for the British or American colonists yet to be overly interested in it, apart from the hope some had of finding a transcontinental river route to the Pacific Ocean—the fabled Northwest Passage, a passage that, if found, would greatly facilitate and increase the lucrative trade with India, China, and Japan.

The American Colonies Following the French and Indian Wars

The defeat of France in the French and Indian Wars, in which Jonathan Carver served as a Massachusetts militiaman, was of momentous significance to the American colonists, greatly influencing the subsequent emergence of the United States as an independent nation. To the British and French governments, the conflict in North America had been only part of their continuing, much wider imperial rivalry. But for the inhabitants of the American colonies, that struggle had been coming of age.

The colonists had not previously been anxious to break their ties with Great Britain. As early as 1754, representatives of the colonies had gathered in Albany and cobbled together a plan of mutual action for frontier defense against the French and their Indian allies. But not one of the colonial assemblies, several of which were perpetually at odds, would then have been willing to ratify such a revolutionary scheme as American unity. They were prepared to raise militia forces to fight, but they preferred to rely on the British colonial authorities to decide how that should be done and to oversee the appropriate arrangements.

When it was later suggested that Americans might unite for an even more important purpose, that of winning their independence from Great Britain, Benjamin Franklin, who would later change his mind, scoffed at the idea. Franklin observed at the time that if the colonies "could not agree to unite for their defense against the French and Indians, who were perpetually harassing their settlements, burning their villages, and murdering their people, can it reasonably be supposed there is any danger of their uniting against their own nation [Great Britain], which protects and encourages them, with which they have so many connections and ties of blood, interest, and affection, and which, it is well known, they all love much more than they love one another?"

But after the decisive, final British triumph over the French in North America, attitudes in the colonies changed. To be under the rule and protection of the British Crown had been comforting and reassuring for the colonists when they had considered themselves threatened. But after France's defeat, such protection was no longer necessary. The Indian tribes, over whose ancestral lands colonial settlements continued to spread, remained a threat on the frontier, but the colonists had actively and ably participated in the struggle against the French and their Indian allies, Colonial frontiersmen had demonstrated greater fighting skills in the wilderness than the British Redcoats. Those professional soldiers had been trained mostly for set-piece confrontations with European adversaries who fought the same way they did; they had not adapted well to frontier-style fighting. They had also never been greatly liked by the colonists, who had often been required to provide for their upkeep.

The colonists emerged from the French and Indian Wars with self-confidence and a greater sense of responsibility for their own well-being than they had ever known before. Those wars proved to be the prologue to the American Revolution. Without them, the Revolution was unlikely to have erupted when it did and American independence might not have been established for some time afterward.

Even so, another dozen years were to pass between the Treaty of Paris and the opening clashes of the Revolution in 1775. Despite vigorous protests in the colonies about restrictive regulations and tax laws imposed by the British Crown, there was, as yet, no determined revolutionary movement. The institutional environment in which the colonists lived still retained powerful and pervasive British undercurrents and overtones. Indeed, for most of the colonists, the British influence largely determined the patterns of their everyday lives.

The law of the colonies was English law. Among other things, it guaranteed its inhabitants freedom of speech, immunity from arbitrary arrest, and trial by jury if charged with a crime. Freedom of the press had been guaranteed by a ruling in a Crown court in New York not long before. The King's English was the predominant language of the colonies. It was the language in which most Americans communicated, conducted business, and prayed. A few years later, the signal that would speed Paul Revere on his way to warn revolutionary militiamen that the Redcoats were coming would be beamed from the steeple of Boston's Anglican North Church. Although the British colonies exercised extensive self-government to a degree totally unknown in colonial possessions of other imperial powers at that time, the senior civil servants in America were dedicated officers of the Crown. Until just before the Revolution, they were commonly respected as such. Far from recognizing the interests they shared in common, each of the thirteen colonies maintained an agent in London, the center of an empire of which they were content to be a part. Each agent promoted his colony's separate interests there, much as states of the Union today commission lobbyists in Washington to be active on their behalf.

Lawyer and poet Francis Hopkinson, who was later one of the signers of the Declaration of Independence, reflected popular opinion in the colonies when he asserted, "We in America are in all respects Englishmen, notwithstanding that the Atlantic rolls her waves between us and the throne to which we all owe allegiance." Benjamin Franklin maintained at the time that he had never "heard in conversation from any person, drunk or sober, the least expression of a wish for a separation, or a hint that such a thing would be advantageous to America."

These attitudes would later be dramatically altered. But such were the prevailing sentiments in 1766 when Jonathan Carver, believing himself to be a properly commissioned agent of the Crown, left his home in Massachusetts and embarked with enthusiasm on an expedition beyond the frontier, into the "interior parts" of America.

Limiting the Expansion Westward

Restlessness had been part of the American character from the very beginning. Barely were the first European settlements established in the New World when some of the colonies moved elsewhere to build new communities. Those, in turn, split up and spawned still others. An English observer noted at the time that, "Wandering about seems engrafted in [the American] nature. They forever imagine that the lands further off are still better than those upon which they are already settled." Daniel Boone would soon push through the Appalachian barrier into the Cumberland Gap of Kentucky. John Sevier, who would later become the first governor of Tennessee, was about to extend his explorations through the wooded landscape of that region. Clear across the frontier, explorers, adventurers, farmers, and hunters probed farther and farther into the western unknown. In 1759, while the Seven Years War was still in progress, French-born Jean de Crevecoeur observed:

> An European, when he first arrives [in the American colonies], seems limited in his intentions, as well as in his views; but he very suddenly alters his scale; two hundred miles formerly appeared a very great distance, it is now but a trifle. He no sooner breathes our air than he forms schemes, and embarks on designs he never would have thought of in his own country. . . . He begins to feel the effects of a sort of resurrection; hitherto he had not lived, but simply vegetated; he now feels himself a man, because he is treated as such; the laws of his own country had overlooked him in his insignificancy; the laws of this cover him with their mantle. Judge what an alteration there must arise in the mind and thoughts of this man. He begins to forget his former servitude and dependence, his heart involuntarily dilates and glows; this first swell inspires him with those new thoughts which constitute an American.

The defeat of the French lent even greater impetus to the American quest for new horizons. A huge expanse of previously disputed land was to be explored, claimed, and tamed. Wealth was to be acquired from speculating in it. George Washington was one of many individuals with an eye to the possibilities, believing that anyone "who neglects the present opportunity of hunting out good lands and in some measure marking and distinguishing them for their own . . . will never regain it." Benjamin Franklin was one of the directors of a company formed to establish a colony on ten million acres of the Ohio Valley. The charters of some of the coastal colonies laid conflicting claim to land "from sea to sea."

For the government in London, the prospect of an uncontrolled surge westward by the impetuous American colonists had few attractions. With the French no longer challenging Britain for supremacy in North America, it had no need for soldier-settlers to move westward to establish a British presence. Nor did added commercial advantage, the Crown's primary interest in the colonies, seem likely to result from settlement farther west. Experience was already showing that even on the seaboard side of the Appalachian barrier, frontier communities tended to be self-sufficient, offering no significant market for British goods.

Gaining dominance over France in North America had proved very expensive for the British Treasury. During the closing years of the conflict, the British national debt had almost doubled. The people of Britain had been led to believe that the wealth to be extracted from the land their nation acquired beyond the seaboard would provide sufficient compensation. But there was as yet no sign that such a reward was being gathered in. On the contrary, although still reeling from the enormous costs of war, the Treasury in London feared it would be pressed to provide resources for the administration of the acquired territory if the colonists were permitted to expand their areas of settlement across it. Garrisons might have to be provided for their protection, and military campaigns might have to be undertaken on their behalf against tribes enraged by the extended colonization of their lands. Some of those tribes had been willing allies of the French during the war because there had been so few French settlers and such little actual expropriation of Indian territory by them.

Ministers of the Crown had no doubt that eventually great wealth was to be gleaned from the trans-Appalachian hinterland. Consideration was given to the establishment of new colonies in the West in due course. But for the moment, they wanted a cooling-off and consolidation period. Hostile tribes in trans-Appalachia were to be given time to settle down and adjust to the changed circumstances.

Expenses incurred in maintaining the security of the colonies were to be trimmed. For those purposes, the British government drew a line on the map, running along the crest of the Appalachian range. Beyond that line, specific royal permission would be required for further settlement. It was not to be lightly given. Indeed, settlers already established beyond the Appalachians were instructed, albeit in vain, to withdraw.

Despite inherent American restlessness, the announcement of this Proclamation Line did not at first arouse as much resentment in the colonies as might have been expected. Its establishment was well received by privileged commercial groups there. Land companies, fur traders, and other merchants, expecting to be officially or unofficially exempted, welcomed the restrictions it imposed on less well connected settlers who might otherwise flood into the western territories, antagonize tribes once more, and intrude upon the privileged positions they themselves intended to establish or had in some cases established already.

Ordinary frontier people were also not overly upset by the establishment of the Proclamation Line. Many were still uncertain about the degree of safety that could be enjoyed beyond the line. Stories of clashes with Indians and of Indian massacres during the war were still fresh in the minds of the colonists, and reports of further incidents were still being received.

But the call of the land beyond the frontier remained overpowering for some Americans. Among them were pioneers who had no intention of obeying decrees issued by authorities far away. Also among them were explorers and adventurers like Jonathan Carver.

Jonathan Carver's Background

The Carvers were among the earliest English settlers in Massachusetts. John Carver, who was the first governor of the Plymouth Colony, the first Pilgrim settlement in New England, is believed to have been Jonathan Carver's great-granduncle. He arrived in North America aboard the Mayflower in 1620, a voyage he was instrumental in organizing. His brother Robert, who is believed to have been Jonathan Carver's great-grandfather, also arrived and settled in Massachusetts early in the seventeenth century.

Jonathan Carver's maternal great-grandfather, Thomas Dyer, was also an early settler in New England. Eliphalet Dyer, one of Jonathan's cousins, was to become a member of the first Continental Congress, and served later as chief justice of Connecticut.

Jonathan Carver's father, Ensign David Carver, was well established in the communities in which the family lived. Among the offices he held at Weymouth were constable and selectman. He also owned property, including a grist mill. When Jonathan was still a boy, the Carvers moved to Canterbury, Connecticut. There, Jonathan's father once again became an important local figure, serving as first selectman (chief administrative officer) and town meeting moderator, as well as holding other public posts. His rank of ensign was an honorary badge of office rather than a military designation. He died when Jonathan was seventeen years old.

Little is known of Jonathan Carver's early years, except that he continued to live in Canterbury upon reaching adulthood. He was married there to Abigail Robbins in 1746. She gave birth to a daughter the following year and another in 1748. Soon afterward—when, exactly, is not known—Jonathan Carver and his family moved to Montague, Massachusetts, eighty miles northwest of Boston. That was where the other Carver children—there were seven in all—were born.

There had been a lull during this time in the British-French contest for dominance in North America, but hostilities were soon resumed. Montague was located in an exposed, sparsely populated region near the frontier of settlement. Beyond it was the wilderness, inhabited by Indians whose amicability could not be counted on. In addition, the town was astride a natural route south from the key French outpost at Montreal.

We do not know how Jonathan Carver earned his living in Massachusetts. There are indications that he may at one stage have been a shoemaker, a craft of much higher status then than now. It was common at the time for young men to be apprenticed to craftsmen, although that did not necessarily prevent them from turning later to other careers. There are suggestions also that Carver may briefly have studied medicine, although there is nothing to indicate that he ever practiced it. That he was chosen a selectman in Montague indicates that he was a figure of some public standing.

Men and women who lived on or near the frontier were required to master many practical skills. They usually built their own homes, provided their own food, and made their own clothes. Whatever their formal callings, their well-being often depended on their ability to coax sustenance and shelter from the land and the woods and to defend themselves by force of arms when necessary. British garrisons were on call to deal with major military crises. But for day-to-day protection, Americans depended on themselves and on locally re-cruited militias in which men, who could not long be spared from their family obligations, enlisted for brief tours of duty.

Records show that Carver was enrolled in a Massachusetts militia unit raised at the town of Deerfield on the frontier in 1755, although he may have served in such a unit even earlier. He was at Fort William Henry on Lake George with a combined British and British American force in 1757 when it was captured by French and Indian forces under General Louis Joseph Montcalm, and where, despite Montcalm's orders, many of the captured soldiers were massacred. Carver himself was being led off into the woods by two Indians to what he presumed would be his death when they released him to pursue a British officer in full uniform, apparently a more tempting victim. Carver escaped with minor wounds.

He served as a second lieutenant in a militia battalion the following year. By 1763, when the French conceded defeat and forfeited their North American territories to the British, Carver had risen to the rank of captain and was commanding a company of militia troops.

Robert Rogers' Attempt to Search
for the Northwest Passage

Among the American frontiersmen who had served with particu-lar distinction in the British American forces during the Seven Years

War was Major Robert Rogers, an important figure in Jonathan Carver's life. Rogers, born in the small frontier town of Methuen, Massachusetts, in 1731, was of Scotch-Irish descent. His parents are believed to have arrived from Northern Ireland only shortly before his birth. His forebears and relatives were simple folk, much less distinguished than those of Carver. He and his parents lived a more precarious life, farming on the New Hampshire frontier. Poverty and French and Indian marauders were a constant threat. When only fourteen years old—old enough on the American frontier in the eighteenth century—Rogers volunteered to serve in the local militia.

For frontiersmen, however, soldiering was never a permanent occupation. They served when needed and returned to cultivation of the land when circumstances permitted. As a young man, Rogers, like others in the frontier, tried his hand at farming. But he soon found himself in financial trouble, unable to pay his debts and implicated in passing counterfeit money. It was evident that he was not temperamentally suited to life on a farm. Unable to stay put and continually venturing into the backcountry, he epitomized early American wanderlust.

When calls for volunteers to fight the French were issued in the colonies in 1755, Rogers, although only twenty-four years old, did more than re-enlist. In what might have been an effort to shield himself against legal proceedings over the counterfeiting charge, he enrolled fifty fellow New Hampshire frontiersmen to serve with him. It was an impressive achievement for so young a man and he was put in charge of those recruits, with the rank of captain.

Unlike most British officers, Rogers took the fight to the enemy regardless of weather conditions or terrain. Tales soon circulated about his exploits in the forests of the hinterland, and newspaper stories about him were written. He became famous throughout the colonies and was awarded official commendations by the British and colonial authorities.

As a result, an "Independent Company of Rangers" was established under his command. It consisted of sixty-five specially recruited fighting men, all experienced in hunting and tracking and capable of enduring long forced marches through wooded country-side. Rogers' Rangers, as they soon came to be called, often fighting behind enemy lines and inflicting severe damage on enemy morale, comprised the first organized corps of elite assault troops in American history. Their youthful commander achieved even greater fame. He was soon promoted to the rank of major.

Although American militia troops did most of the fighting in the French and Indian Wars, the British considered the American troops less reliable than their own. Many British officers were openly contemptuous of the Americans. But although many considered Rogers a boorish yokel and widely criticized the lack of traditional forms of discipline in the ranks of the Rangers, their achievements were for the most part much admired by the British command. After the French defeat, Rogers was entrusted with undertaking the still dangerous task of venturing deep into newly won former French territory to take possession of wilderness outposts, most notably Detroit.

The daring with which Rogers performed his military missions and the acclaim he received were, however, overshadowed by personal problems. He was deeply in debt. He had borrowed from money lenders not only for his own needs and speculations, but to advance pay to the men under his command, some of whom were now dead. He could get little satisfaction from the British command on that score, partly because he had kept inadequate accounting records. He was also implicated in a number of bad financial deals. In 1764, on the complaint of a creditor, he was committed to prison in New York, from which he was forcibly freed by men of the First Battalion of the Royal Americans, who were offended that so dedicated and popular an officer should be treated so shabbily.

Unable to resolve his difficulties, Rogers looked to London for respite and a change of circumstances. In 1765, he crossed the Atlantic in an attempt to exploit his fame, which had spread to England. He intended to offer his services to the Crown on a mission that, in addition to clearing his debts, would gain him both fortune and further renown—a major expedition to locate and trace the Northwest Passage, a navigable waterway across North America to the Pacific Ocean. He had "a Moral certainty" that such a route existed.

The discovery of a Northwest Passage had long been a dream of merchants contemplating the fortunes that could be generated by far easier and quicker access to the riches of the Far East than the immensely long voyages from Europe by ship around the southern tips of Africa or South America. Explorers had long sought such a passage across North America.

For Rogers, hope of succeeding where others had failed was stirred by his adventures in the American backcountry during the war, and not least by the reward of twenty thousand pounds the British Admiralty had offered. He sought authorization from the Crown to undertake an expedition "for the benefit and Advantage of the British Interests in that Wide-Spread Empire, which the Glorious Successes of the Late War added to His Majesty's Dominions." According to his plan, his three-year exploration would lead him first to the Mississippi, and then "to the River called by the Indian Ouragon, which flows into a Bay that projects North-Easterly into the Country from the Pacific Ocean." For the expedition, Rogers wanted two hundred officers and men, as well as sufficient funds to provide adequate supplies, including presents to propitiate Indians across whose lands he would have to travel.

By virtue of his wartime exploits, Rogers was able to gain the backing of several influential figures in London, including the prominent politician Charles Townshend, member of the Board of Trade William Fitzherbert, and the Lord Mayor of London. If his proposed expedition had not seemed so costly, he might well have received full authorization. He was given encouragement by being offered the position of "Governor Commandant of His Majesty's Garrison at Michilimakana"—the fort at Michilimackinac, present-day Mackinac in Michigan, which had only shortly before been acquired from the French. He was also awarded the honor of being presented at court to King George III. But allocation of the necessary funding for his proposed expedition was not forthcoming. Insisting that North American costs were to be sharply curtailed now that the war with France was over, the Treasury recoiled at the idea of substantial expenditures of the kind Rogers was proposing.

Nevertheless, Rogers was advised by his influential London patrons to take the post he had been offered at Michilimackinac. They said his appointment to it was proof that the Crown was impressed with his zeal and determination to seek out the Northwest Passage; moreover, the appointment suggested that allocation of the requested funds for the expedition, for which in any case Michilimackinac was the intended initial forward base, was likely to be forthcoming in due course. Besides, as commandant there, Rogers, who had creditors with whom to settle up, would at least have a paying job.

In the end Rogers was persuaded. It seemed likely to him either that he would gain eventual approval from the Crown for his proposed cross-country expedition, or that an unauthorized search for a Northwest Passage would subsequently earn him such great acclaim that it was worth embarking on regardless. Consequently, upon his return to America, he commissioned several people to assist him in the project. Among them was Jonathan Carver.

Carver and Rogers did not know each other well, although it is possible that they had met during the period of their military service. Carver certainly knew of Rogers' well-publicized achievements in the war. Upon learning that this famous frontiersman had requested officials of the Crown in London to authorize an expedition into the interior, he had offered his services. Although Carver was already fifty-six years old and only a self-taught map maker, he had, as he told Rogers, "studiously endeavoured to inform [himself] in every science necessary for a compleet draughts man." He had journeyed extensively through New England and nearby parts of Canada and had drawn maps of the region. In need of a map maker to chart his expedition, Rogers took Carver on not expressly to find a Northwest Passage, but merely "to explore the interior and unknown Tracts of the Continent of America at the back of Your Majesty's Colonies, and to Inspect the same and make Observations, Surveys and Draughts thereof." It is possible that Carver did not at first know that Rogers had far greater aspirations than that.

Carver later suggested that it was patriotism that had motivated him to undertake his journey into the interior. In his introduction to *Travels,* he wrote that at the conclusion of the war with France, during which he had "rendered my country some services," he pondered how he might continue to be of service. He wished, he said, to help Great Britain derive advantage from its acquisition of vast additional territory in North America by providing greater awareness of what that territory consisted of and contained.

Carver may indeed have genuinely wished to serve the interests of the Crown. He was undoubtedly a loyal American subject of the king. His public service in Massachusetts and in the militia suggests that he was a man of principle, reliability, and achievement. There is no doubt that he, like Rogers, had a restless nature and that he was greatly attracted to opportunities that might exist on and beyond the colonial frontier. He had already unsuccessfully applied to the Massachusetts Bay House of Representatives for the position of commander of an outpost in the wilds of Maine.

But the prospect of financial reward no doubt played a central role in Carver's calculations. He was in great need of gainful employment. Regular British Army officers, known as The Establishment, had special privileges. Those who retired in North America, including American-born officers, were entitled to pensions of half-pay and grants of land. As a volunteer militiaman, Carver had no such entitlements and had little to fall back on when the war with France was over. A married man with a family, he could not afford to undertake a long, expensive mission without backing. No matter how dedicated he was to public service, it is likely that he ventured into the interior on the expedition that was to make him posthumously famous only because he believed that Robert Rogers had actually received authorization for it from the Crown and that he would be paid by the British Treasury.

Despite the impression given in his book, Carver was by no means the key individual in the enterprise. Rogers was its organizer and central figure. But he would be able to oversee it only from a distance, at least during its opening phase. If the Crown signaled its authorization for his scheme and provided the funds and personnel he requested, he might take direct command. But until that happened, he would be required to remain restlessly stuck at Fort Michilimackinac, seeing to his duties there.

Rogers commissioned Captain James Tute, a former Ranger and one of his most trusted and resourceful subordinates during the Seven Years War, to lead the expedition in the field. Tute was to command "a Party for the Discovery of the North West Passage from the Atlantick into the Passifick Ocean if any such passage there be, or for the discovery of the great river Ourigan that falls into the Pacifick Ocean about Latitude Fifty." Tute was instructed to be careful not to offend the tribes whose territories the expedition crossed. He was to pay punctually for anything received from them and he was not to "take" their women without the consent of their chiefs.

James Stanley Goddard, another former officer and a trader in the hinterland, was appointed by Rogers to be Tute's "secretary for Indian affairs," and was to be second in command. Although Carver's role in the expedition was important, and he was to precede the others in the trek westward, he was signed on only as draftsman and map maker, and was third in command.

Carver's Explorations

Setting off from Boston on May 20, 1766, Carver made for Michilimackinac by way of Albany, Oswego, Niagara, and Fort Detroit, recording his observations in his journal as he proceeded. He noted, for example, that "The sand about Detroit is very good for Agriculture tho some lyes a little to low yet this will serve for good grass and pastur land and nothing seems to be wanting but good farmers to possess it."

Although comparatively modest in size, Michilimackinac was an important British outpost and trading center. Overlooking the straits between Lake Huron and Lake Michigan, the fort was a French-built stockaded enclosure that contained, in addition to accommodations for the commandant and a small garrison of troops, a few houses belonging to fur traders. Now that the wars were over, it was hardly a place of excitement. Elizabeth Rogers, who accompanied her husband when he took command of the fort, had an appalling time there. She later wrote: "To paint in their true colors my sufferings during my stay in that remote and lonely region would be a task beyond my ability." But Michilimackinac, strategically situated, was a gateway to the northwestern wilderness and a base for contact with Indian nations whose allegiance the British now sought.

Such allegiance could not be presupposed, as the uprising led by Pontiac, a charismatic chief of the Ottawa tribe, had demonstrated in 1763. Despite the Treaty of Paris, the French still encouraged tribes that had been allies to stand ready to resume the fight against the British and British Americans, whom they described, with some justification, as "a Quareling People and always divided among themselves."

Carver arrived at Michilimackinac on August 28, 1766, and formally received his commission from "Robert Rogers Esqr. Agent to the Western Indians and Governor Commandant of His Majesty's Garrison." He was directed to "set out from this post emmediently." With the help of previously drawn maps, mostly the work of French explorers and believed to be of limited reliability, he was to proceed through Lake Michigan to Green Bay and then, by way of the Fox and Wisconsin rivers to the Mississippi, along which he was to ascend as far as the Falls of St. Anthony, at the site of present-day Minneapolis. That was expected to be the farthest extent of his journey before winter set in. He was to make "an exact plan of the countery by the way marking down all Indian towns with their numbers, as also to take survaies of the diffrant posts, lakes, and rivers as also the mountains."

Carver was to winter in the area, and in the spring he was to dispatch a written report to Rogers at Michilmackinac by one of the traders who regularly traversed the region. Instructions for him to continue farther westward might be sent to him. If he received none, he was to return to the fort by way of the Illinois and St. Joseph rivers to Lake Michigan and then along the lake's eastern shore, mapping the area and keeping detailed records of all he saw. He was to be paid eight shillings a day, "together with other incidental charges." On September 3, having gathered the necessary supplies, Carver set off to fulfill this assignment.

There was nothing in Carver's commission to suggest that this was to be the opening phase of a much wider expedition to seek the Northwest Passage. It is possible that he did not know about that objective at the time. In the instructions Rogers issued to James Tute nine days later, however, the search for the passage was clearly spelled out. Tute was to catch up with Carver at the Falls of St. Anthony and take him under his command. Rogers later said that he had by then received news from London encouraging him to believe that Crown authorization for his ambitious quest would soon be forthcoming.

Setting off from Michilimackinac, Carver, joining a party of fur traders heading west, proceeded by canoe to Green Bay and then along the Fox River. That route took him to "the great town of the Winnebagoes," situated on an island in Lake Winnebago, presided over by an amiable elderly woman who seemed to be a figurehead rather than actual chief. Authority appeared to reside in a venerable relative of hers, who struck Carver as being "a very good humoured sensible old man."

Carver and the party with which he was traveling were received with "great civility." He conferred with elders of the tribe and was given permission to pass through their territory. He was greatly impressed with the richness of the soil, the fertility of the region, and the variety of crops—including Indian corn, wild rice, beans, squash, grapes, and plums—either cultivated by the Indians or growing naturally. He was much taken also with the great numbers and variety of fish and birds.

From the town of the Winnebagoes, he and his party continued up the Fox River to the so-called Carrying Place. There the canoes had to be portaged—lifted from the water and borne overland—partly through tall grass, partly across a plain, for almost two miles to the Wisconsin River. A day's travel up the Wisconsin took them to another Indian community, "the Great Town of the Saukies" (the Sauk Indians). With its well-built wooden houses of neatly jointed hewn planks, straight and spacious streets, and tidily laid out, productive farm gardens, it appeared to Carver and those with whom he traveled to be "more like a civilized town than the abode of savages."

After a brief stay there, he and his party proceeded downriver. They reached the Mississippi at Prairie du Chien, a large Indian market town where traders from many tribes, including some whose territory was a good distance off, congregated each May for barter. There Carver parted with the men whose journey from Michilimackinac he had shared. They intended to camp nearby for the winter to await the spring and the trading opportunities that would be available then. Carver purchased a canoe in order to continue his voyage of discovery. He fixed a pipe of peace to the head of it to signal his amicable intentions and flew a Union Jack from its stern. With two men he hired, a French Canadian and a Mohawk Indian, he set off up the Mississippi, exploring its banks as he proceeded.

His small party experienced a number of adventures en route, including a brush with a group of Indian renegades, outcasts from their various tribes, who had banded together for purposes of plunder. He stumbled across what appeared to be the remains of manmade riverside fortifications several centuries old. He successfully interceded to avert a clash between two rival bands of Indians.

Carver was compelled by threatening water conditions to proceed overland along the Mississippi to the Falls of St. Anthony. He explored the region around "this astonishing work of nature" before continuing upriver. He proceeded as far as the mouth of the St. Francis River above the falls, observing deer, beavers, and otters in such profusion that, he remarked, no hunter would fail to return from the area "loaded beyond his expectation."

By then, severe winter weather was setting in and Carver considered it advisable to backtrack to the mouth of the Minnesota River, which was then called the River St. Pierre, along which he proceeded westward in search of a winter refuge. On December 7, 1766, he reached a village of Dakota Sioux Indians. In his journal and book, he calls them the "Naudowessies," which is probably what the members of this community of Sioux called themselves. He was received cautiously at first. But assured of his amicable intentions, the Naudowessies permitted him to take up residence among them. It was an exciting and enriching experience for both him and them. He was soon accepted as a friend, and great hospitality was extended to him through the long winter. Before he left the Sioux village in the spring, he was made an honorary chief.

The notations Carver made in his journal while on the expedition were roughly jotted down and were sometimes a mere scrawl, lacking the punctuation and penmanship niceties of their subsequent revision. But they were often remarkably detailed:

> The Naudowessee in their manner of government differ in some respects from the other Nations of Indians and may more properly be calld a Common Wealth or Republick they are Divided into bands to each of which they have given Distinguishing names as we do to regiments. The Chiefs of these Bands are hereditary in their families Besides these every band has a chiefe who is calld the Chief of the Warriors whose office does not Decend to him in his family but is Chosen by the people or ascends to it by merit He never goes out to war but orders all the departments destind against the Enemy and gives them their Routs and particular instructions as far as is Needfull there is another Chief in Each Band who is calld the second Chief of the Warriors he goes out with the party and they obey him as their Commander, This officer governs the Soldiers in camp, these soldiers are always kept up and are armd in Readiness to go at a Minuts Notice on any Emergency whatever.

In addition to commenting on the structure of Sioux society, Carver described many of the traditions, customs, and personal habits of the Indians he stayed with:

> Their marriage customs are very peculiar, when two young people are about to joyn in Wedlock they walk out both together on the parade which is generally in the Middle of the Camp where a number assembles to assist in the ceremony among these is one of their under chiefs who in a Short Speech informs the Spectators that them two calling over their names are come there that the whole may witness that they love each other that he takes her for his Wife (which they Call Tak-

shedigo) to get wood dress his victuals take care of the Tent both while
he is at home and out a hunting and at war, after which they take hold
of Each others' hand and the whole of the spectators Discharge their
arrows over the heads of the Bride and Bridegroom after which the
man turns his back to the Bride She gets on him and he carrys her to
his tent the spectators give a Loud Cohoop and wish them happy all
their days thus ends the ceremony

Carver's Journal of His Travels

According to the instructions Robert Rogers had issued, Tute,
Goddard, and Carver, unless told otherwise, were to resume their
explorations in the spring. They were to proceed by river and overland into the northwest with the aid of Sioux guides. Rogers was
supposed to arrange for essential supplies to catch up with them on
their travels. If the supplies did not arrive, they were to consider
themselves authorized to issue IOUs in Rogers' name as commandant
at Michilimackinac for the purchase of goods and merchandise from
traders they might meet and for the payment of Indian guides they
might employ. They would find their way to the "great River
Ouregan" which, Rogers believed, "emtys into the Pacefick Occian."

Things went wrong practically from the beginning. Tute and
Goddard were unable to get as far as the Falls of St. Anthony to join
Carver by the time winter set in. That proved fortunate for Carver,
as without his associates, he had far more intimate contact with the
Sioux than he otherwise might have enjoyed.

It was during those winter months that he learned about their tribal
and family structure, the relations between the men and women, their
religious beliefs and practices, their ways of hunting and cultivating
the land, their ancestral enemies, how they made war and peace, what
games they played, their food and attire, and much more. He learned
enough of their language to enable him to converse with them and to
help him subsequently compose a basic Naudowessie-English dictionary.

When spring arrived, Carver took ceremonial leave of his hosts.
After a mostly friendly encounter with Chippewa Indians en route,
he returned to the trading village of Prairie du Chien, where he was

able finally to join up with Tute and Goddard. It soon became clear that the expedition was in trouble.

In a message from Michilimackinac, Rogers had warned Tute not to encourage Indians to believe he was anything but a humble trader. Otherwise, he had been told, he would be assumed to be a "great man" and expected to distribute presents beyond his means. But another task the members of the expedition had been instructed to undertake contradicted that warning and precluded penny-pinching. They were to convince the Indians that, contrary to French suggestions, the British meant them no harm and were instead their dedicated friends. They were to persuade them to look upon Fort Michilimackinac as a major trading center where their dealings with the British would prove both lucrative and agreeable.

Seeking to make those points and, at the same time, to assure themselves of the good will and assistance of the Indians for their further travels, they lavishly distributed gifts. That caused problems. In addition to infuriating the white traders congregated at Prairie du Chien for the spring market, who were expected by the Indians to match their generosity, it almost exhausted their resources.

Instead of proceeding with their westward trek, they therefore set off by way of the Chippewa and St. Croix rivers for Grand Portage on Lake Superior, where they hoped arrangements had already been made to have their store of supplies replenished. But instead of supplies, Tute received a message from Rogers complaining of his extravagance and expressing fears that he, Rogers, might be financially ruined unless his team of explorers already had sufficient supplies to complete their expedition.

Carver later sought to justify how liberally the gifts had been distributed. He said the Indians were being assiduously courted by the French and the Spanish. He wrote that "anyone well acquainted with the circumstances of the Indians on the Mississippi in the beginning of the year 1767 will say that they are of the Opinion that if it had not been for the Pains taken by Capt Tute and Mr. Goddard and myself by Loading on them with presents beyond what would need have been given in any other Case," many of the tribes, including the Sioux, whose friendship was sought would have been dangerously alienated. The members of the expedition did not risk remaining long at Grand Portage to await reprovisioning, which was in any case uncertain. Nor could they consider attempting to reach the far-off "Pacefick Ocean." Disappointed, but aware of the stark realities of their situation, they aborted their expedition in the autumn of 1767 and returned to Michilimackinac to sort matters out with Rogers and to winter there.

The failure to come anywhere near finding a Northwest Passage, or even the slightest evidence that such a route actually existed, was a great setback for Rogers. He had hoped that the unauthorized expedition would lead to renewed fame and fortune, but he had no funds with which to revive it. Carver must also have deeply regretted how things had turned out. He might not have known earlier about the ultimate goal of the task for which he had been commissioned, but by this time he was certainly aware of it and must have been disappointed that the search for a transcontinental waterway was being called off. He was being denied the opportunity of participating in a momentous discovery.

Nevertheless, he felt greatly rewarded by his observations and experiences in the wilderness and among the people whose home it was. He had met Indians of various tribes. In addition to having lived among the Sioux and (more briefly) the Chippewa, he had learned about some of the ways of the Winnebagoes, the Assiniboins, the Kilistinons, the Sauks, and the Foxes. While at Michilimackinac, he wrote a long letter to his wife recounting some of his adventures and observations:

My Dear—I arrived at this place the 30th of last month [August 1767] from the westward; last winter I spent among the Naudoussee of the Plains, a roving nation of Indians, near the river St. Piere, one of the western branches of the Mississippi, near fourteen hundred miles west of Michillimacinac. This nation live in bands, and continually march like the roving Arabians in Asia. They live in tents of leather and are very powerful. I have learned and procured a specimen of their dialect and to the utmost of my power, have made minute remarks on their customs and manners, and likewise of many other nations that I have passed through; which I dare say, you and my

26

acquaintances will think well worth hearing, and which I hope (by the continuation of the same divine Providence that has hitherto in this my journeying, in a most remarkable manner, guarded over me in all my ways) personally to communicate. It would require a volume to relate all the hardships and dangers I have suffered since I left you, by stormy tempests on these lakes and river, by hunger and cold, in danger of savage beasts, and men more savage than they.

Some of the stories Carver recounted to his wife in his letter would be repeated and expanded in his book when it appeared. Of the religious beliefs of the Indians he came to know, he told her, "They believe there is a superior spirit, or God, who is infinitely good, and that there is a bad spirit, or devil. When they are in trouble, they pray to the devil, because they say, that God, being good, will not hurt them, but the evil spirit that hurts them, can only avert their misery."

The letter was optimistic. Carver appeared to be very pleased with himself for having been involved in and having survived a hazardous but fascinating enterprise. He had no complaints. He said he looked forward to being home again and to receiving recompense for his labors.

He and the others were not yet aware that Rogers had never received the Crown's authorization for his ambitious endeavor and that he was unable to live up to his commitments to them. They did not know that they would not be paid. Nor did they yet know about discord between Rogers and Sir William Johnson, superintendent of Indians in the region. Johnson, a man who jealously guarded his authority, did not like Rogers. He felt aggrieved because he had not been consulted by London about Rogers' appointment as commandant at Michilimackinac. He objected to the bills that were accumulating for expenditures at the fort for supplies and presents for Indians. He had instructed Benjamin Roberts, one of his officials, to be especially diligent in overseeing the handling of the fort's accounts. A feud had long existed between Roberts and Rogers. Friction between them was inevitable and created an atmosphere of intrigue at the fort that further fueled Johnson's animosity toward its commandant.

Rogers had a high-handed way of doing things. He also had a quick temper and a knack for making enemies. Among those he made at Michilimackinac was one of his own appointees, a former officer named Nathaniel Potter. Potter told Benjamin Roberts that Rogers was planning to desert to the French or the Spanish and hand the fort over to them. Emissaries of several tribes had converged on the fort to signify their friendship with the British, a major success for Rogers on behalf of the Crown. But Potter suggested that courting the tribes might have been part of Rogers' plot.

Although without substantiation, the accusation was a serious one in view of British uncertainty about security in the newly acquired west country. It brought matters to a head at Michilimackinac. Without being aware of it, Rogers was formally charged with conspiring to hand the fort over to the enemy, as well as with embezzling public property. In December 1767, while Carver was there awaiting the arrival of spring to head for home, orders arrived for Rogers to be removed from command and arrested for treason. To Rogers' astonishment, he was arrested without warning on the fort's parade ground, put in irons, and placed in solitary confinement. When weather conditions permitted, he was to be taken to the British garrison at Montreal for court martial.

The arrest of Rogers, and the disclosure that he had had no official authorization to mount the expedition, was a shock to Carver. He had been counting on the money that he believed was due him, and perhaps other benefits as well. He had told his wife that Rogers had promised to "take special care to acquaint the Government . . . of my services." He now realized that Rogers could not even fulfill his contractual obligation to pay him the promised eight shillings a day—now amounting to a substantial sum—and that the Crown was under no obligation to do so either.

Carver appealed to General Thomas Gage, the British military commander in America. Gage was sympathetic. He was prepared to certify that there was no reason to disbelieve Carver's account of his travels or of the hardships he had endured on them. But he emphasized that Great Britain could not be held responsible for commitments that Rogers, the alleged traitor, had made without authorization.

Carver must have felt particularly bitter during those last winter weeks at Michilimackinac. There was no financial reward or recognition for the work to which he had devoted more than two years, and he had no other prospects of employment. He must have spent much of his time while waiting for the weather to turn wondering what he could do to reverse the bleakness of his circumstances. By the spring, when he was able to trek back to Massachusetts, he appeared to have decided on a plan for raising money to support himself and his family and at the same time to gain recognition for his labors and achievements.

During the dismal winter at Michilimackinac, Carver completed work on the journal of his travels. He wrote well and with precision. The journal was full of details about the quality and character of the terrain of the American hinterland and about the ways of the people who lived beyond the frontier, subjects of great interest throughout the colonies. Stories, speculation, and rumors abounded, but the public had access to comparatively little factual information. There was reason to believe that if the journal were published, there would be a ready market for it. At worst, it might reimburse him to some degree for the time and effort he had expended on the expedition.

There is evidence that Carver's travels were not without interest to the general public. On August 8, 1768, shortly after his return from the wilds, the *Boston Chronicle* contained a report about his activities and movements:

> Captain Carver, formerly of the New-England troops, arrived at Philadelphia on the 24th of July last from Fort Pitt, and informs us, that the garrison were very healthy about a fortnight ago. This gentleman has been employed several years as a draughtsman, and has been exploring the heads of the Mississippi, the Scioto, and Lake Superior, in which service he has given great satisfaction, having made several discoveries of considerable utility.

Such newspaper accounts were gratifying, but Carver discovered that publishing his journal required funds, and he had none to spare. At the time, it was not unusual for authors and publishers to call on potential readers to finance such projects. Accordingly, on September 12, 1768, an advertisement appeared in the *Boston Chronicle:*

JONATHAN CARVER

Formerly a Captain in the provincial troops of the
Massachusetts-Bay, during the late war in America, and
since employed as a surveyor and draughtsman in
exploring the interior and upper parts of the continent
adjoining to, and beyond lake Superior, and to the
westward of the great river Mississippi, offers the
following

PROPOSALS TO THE PUBLIC,

To publish, as soon as a proper number
of subscribers encourage him in the design,
An EXACT JOURNAL of his TRAVELS
In the years 1766 and 1767,
In which time he travelled upwards of 2500 miles, among
the remote nations of Indians, many of whom had never
before seen a white person.

This JOURNAL will also contain Descriptions of the Indian nations—Of their manners and customs—Of the soil and produce of the country—Of the great lakes Huron, Michigan, and Superior, &c. &c. &c.—Of the Mississippi and other great rivers that run in that part of the continent; and in particular, a full account of the Naudowesse Indians, the most numerous nation of Indians in North-America, who live in tents of leather, and can raise 6000 fighting men, and among whom the author wintered in 1766.

DRAUGHTS and *PLANS* of these countries will be annexed, together with curious figures of the Indian tents, arms, and of the Buffaloe Snake which they worship.

Each Subscriber to pay *Two Spanish Dollars** for every copy of the proposed work; and as soon as a sufficient number have subscribed, to indemnify the expence of the printing and engraving, the publication will immediately ensue.

SUBSCRIPTIONS are taken in by Capt. CARVER at MONTAGUE, and by J. Mein, at the LONDON BOOK-STORE North-side of King-street BOSTON.

---

* A severe shortage of coins in the English Colonies led to the adoption of the Spanish milled dollar from the Caribbean islands as commonly used currency. It later was the standard for the United States silver dollar.

Carver evidently considered it prudent not to seek advantage from publicly linking himself with Robert Rogers, who was still awaiting trial and whose reputation was much tarnished. Such a precaution, however, did not seem to make much difference. It is not known how many people were willing to invest two Spanish dollars in his opus, but the journal was not published, indicating that the response to the advertisement must have been discouraging.

Carver, however, did not give up hope of receiving from the British government the remuneration he had been promised by Rogers for his part in the expedition. Despite the intensifying discontent that the British government's high-handedness was provoking in the colonies, many Americans still had great faith in the fairness of the Crown and its officials. It was not unusual for a colonist who failed in a petition for justice at home to carry his appeal to a higher authority in London, and that is what Carver decided to do: petition the Crown for reimbursement for the time and energy expended on his westward trek. He also may have believed that it would be easier to publish his journal in England. The British capital was more of a literary center than Boston, and fascination with the American hinterland was widespread there as well.

Traveling to England would offer Carver an additional opportunity. Having probed the North American interior, and having lived for a while among Indians, he considered himself well suited for an appointment as a Crown administrator of Indian territories newly acquired from France. He would be better able to petition the Crown for such a position when he was in London.

This was six years before the American Revolution erupted. No one—not even George Washington, Thomas Jefferson, or any of the others who would lead the independence movement—yet suspected that the British colonies would soon attempt to detach themselves from the mother country by force of arms, and that they would succeed in doing so.

Carver had other concerns. His situation appeared to have turned desperate. The North Atlantic is turbulent in winter, but he did not wait until the spring brought calmer waters. He set sail in February

1769, comforted by the news that Robert Rogers had been acquitted at his trial in Montreal for lack of evidence. Carver's petition for reimbursement from the Crown therefore probably would not be jeopardized by the association with Rogers.

Carver left his family behind in New England. He does not appear to have made provision for their well-being. That may have been because he was impoverished and unable to do so. The letter he had written to his wife from Michilimackinac indicated a close and fond relationship between them. He had told his wife at the time that he longed to see her and their children. His closing salutation to Abigail Carver in that letter was "your's forever."

He may have intended to concern himself with her welfare and that of his children once his plans had come to fruition in England. But there is no evidence either of that or of a deliberate rupture between them. They may have subsequently corresponded. But after his departure for England, neither his wife nor their children ever saw him again. Records indicate that Abigail Carver kept a summer school in Montague, Massachusetts, in 1770, at a time when her husband was pleading in London for recompense from the Crown. That suggests she earned a living as a teacher. She died in 1802, and is buried in Brandon, Vermont.

Carver in London

Carver was already fifty-nine years old when he reached London, but England was for him potentially the land of opportunity. It was there, he felt, that his exertions in the American interior would receive the reward they merited. It was there that he would be able to publish his journal of explorations and that he would finally be paid for his services to the Crown.

London was an exciting place for an American. Compared to the British capital, American cities, for all their bursting energy, were unsophisticated and unworldly. London was a dazzling metropolis, a center of culture and taste with wonderful things to see and do. Many of the attractions the British capital offers today were attractions even then, including the British Museum, Westminster Abbey, and the Tower of London, where, at the time, a zoo of exotic animals was in residence. Other curiosities to fascinate a visiting American included public hangings, which always drew large crowds, and a range of theatrical presentations that audiences would attend armed with rotten fruit, ready to make their views tellingly known if they judged a performance to be less than enthralling.

Although he was hopeful, Carver could not have been certain how he would be received in the mother country. British feelings about the American colonists were mixed. For some Britons, their transatlantic cousins were a fascinating breed, continually facing and meeting adventures and challenges. They tamed the wild frontier and amassed fortunes in the counting houses of Philadelphia or on Virginia plantations. Even people with limited aspirations could be tantalized by the land of opportunity across the Atlantic where, it was said, everyone could find land and employment. In his panegyric on life on the American frontier, Jean de Crevecoeur had told them, "Whatever be his talents or inclinations, if they are moderate, [a person] may satisfy them [in America]."

But others in Great Britain, particularly those among the elite, saw the colonists as the coarsest of provincials, bereft of good taste, good manners, and good judgment. Wit and sophisticate Samuel Johnson quipped, "I am willing to love all mankind, except an American."

Regardless of what they thought of the colonies and the colonists, the British generally objected to the great cost of defending them from the French for so long. They bridled at the continuing expense of maintaining armed forces in the colonies for the benefit of their inhabitants. And now the thankless colonists were noisily objecting to comparatively minor burdens imposed on them to help Great Britain shoulder the great financial burden of maintaining an empire— impositions like a stamp tax and a smattering of trade restrictions. The prerevolutionary Sons of Liberty were presuming to hound and harass officials of the Crown in the colonies, on some occasions going so far as to tar and feather them and run them out of town.

Not all colonists were considered responsible for such ingratitude.

Many Americans were seen in Britain as good and loyal subjects of the king, properly appreciative of the mother country and what it had to offer. Well-to-do colonists sent their offspring to London to be properly educated. Many of the most eminent physicians and lawyers in the colonies had been trained in England and could not imagine themselves as being anything but British Americans. Even John Hancock, whose signature would be first on the Declaration of Independence, had chosen to spend time in England to sharpen his business skills when he was a young, aspiring entrepreneur. Several worthy colonists had taken up more or less permanent residence in London. Among them were distinguished, well-connected figures like Benjamin Franklin. One of them, Henry Cruger of New York, had even become a member of Parliament.

Carver, who arrived in the British capital knowing no one and short of cash, was fortunate to have an introduction to Franklin from Samuel Cooper, a prominent Boston preacher. Franklin, who had been representing the interests of several of the American colonies in London, was much admired there and traveled in distinguished circles. Carver impressed him greatly with his account of his travels, and Franklin promised to help him if he could.

It is not known what efforts Franklin made along those lines. He may have introduced Carver to some well-placed Englishmen who could lend him encouragement and perhaps put in a good word for him in official circles. Carver is known to have been befriended by a number of eminent figures in London, including the prominent physician Dr. John Fothergill and Sir Joseph Banks, president of the Royal Society, to whom his book would later be dedicated.

Carver was to have difficulty, however, gaining the sympathy and support of the Crown. British policies with regard to the trans-Appalachian region were still being debated by ministers and officials. They had not yet decided how to exploit their territorial acquisitions to best advantage. Nor had they determined how best to go about maintaining or establishing satisfactory relations with Indian tribes. Now that the French no longer posed a serious threat, some of the colonial administrators recoiled against the practice of plying Indians with gifts to gain or retain their friendship, while others insisted that it was essential to continue to do so, for humanitarian reasons as well as reasons of state. Established codes of gift giving and gift receiving played an important role in each tribe's relations with others. For the British, these were complicated matters, involving both present expenditure and future return.

Socially and financially, Carver was a figure of little significance in London. He also had no notable political patrons there. The British authorities were deeply suspicious of individuals who chose to probe the American interior without having received the Crown's permission. They considered them to be self-seeking adventurers who took little account of the possibly damaging consequences of their actions. Unless Carver could make a respectable case for himself, he was in danger of having his claim for recompense for his explorations summarily dismissed.

Soon after arriving in London, he presented his petition to the Crown, "praying his Majesty to take his case into consideration and afford him some recompense for his service and expence in exploring the interior and unfrequented parts of America." His claim was spelled out in considerable detail and aroused sufficient interest for him to be permitted to put his argument to the British Board of Trade on July 4, 1769. He presented to its members the written commission he had received from Rogers for payment of eight shillings a day while he performed the duties to which he had been assigned. To that he added a sum for incidental expenses he had incurred. As evidence of the extent and value of his labors, he submitted his journal and maps.

Carver must have been encouraged to have gotten that far so quickly. But after examining the claim he presented, the board rejected it. "We are inclined to think," it announced, "that no discoveries of general and national importance appear to have been made." It said, "the Petitioner having engaged in this Expedition under a Commission from Major Rogers, which that officer was by no means authorized to grant, He cannot now by virtue of such an appointment make any regular Claim or demand for indemnification for his labour and expences."

Nevertheless, the authorities had been impressed with Carver's zeal, efforts, and good intentions, and with the character references he submitted. General Gage, the British military commander in America, had written that he had served the Crown in the war "with Reputation, and has ever bore the Character of a very good Man." Massachusetts-born Brigadier General Timothy Ruggles wrote that Carver had "always behaved with Bravery, Fidelity, Humanity & Decorum, and ever approved himself to his superior Officers." The distinguished English friends Carver had made may also have been able to intercede on his behalf.

In any case, he was adjudged by the authorities to have "acquitted himself in His Majesty's Service with reputation and fidelity" and an *ex gratia* payment on compassionate grounds was offered, provided he submitted his "Maps Charts plans Discoveries and observations" to the Board of Trade. A report from London in the *Boston News-Letter* suggested that he was required to hand them over so that the Spanish "who are making themselves formidable at the mouth of the Mississippi, will be prevented from obtaining that knowledge of the heads of that vast river, and the continent thereabouts, which otherwise they would have done, had those journals been made public."

The order that he deliver his expedition documents to the authorities if he wished to be treated sympathetically presented Carver with a problem. He had already put them in the hands of a bookseller who had plans for their publication in book form. Carver was able to retrieve them in due course and "chearfully" hand them over, although he was careful to keep copies. But the promised recompense from the Crown remained limited to little more than the equivalent of the expenses he had incurred on his travels.

Several months later, he spelled out his claim once more to the Lords Commissioners of His Majesty's Treasury. He told them he found himself "reduced to great Want and distress." His subsequent petitions grew even more impassioned as he recounted once more his

"Fatiguing and dangerous travel into the interior Country of North America." Carver claimed that he had penetrated farther than any English subject or even French explorer had before. He suggested that he was prepared to accept less than the sum for which he had originally petitioned. He also indicated that he was planning to return to the colonies once his claim had been granted.

Although he did not return to America, it is possible that some sort of sum may indeed have been awarded to him. Otherwise it is difficult to see how he could have sustained himself in England as the months and then the years slipped by. In an appeal to the Crown for recompense in 1773, he claimed to have been "without pay or Employment" for three years. Bemoaning his circumstances in a petition to the Earl of Dartmouth, the British Secretary of State for America, he pleaded for an appointment to a position, "Civil or Military," that would take him back to the colonies. He wrote that "from his great acquaintance and Extensive Knowledge of the Manners, Customs, and Languages of those interiour Indians," he could be "very usefull to the public if Employed as an Agent for Indian Affairs." He observed that tribal chiefs had complained to him "that they were not well known or properly Represented to their Great Father the English King."

Carver submitted that he was admirably suited to make good that shortcoming and, at the same time, use his experience and skills to increase transatlantic trade to the benefit of British merchants. His circumstances increasingly desperate, he would have been pleased to have been offered any even halfway suitable position, perhaps as a surveyor or draughtsman. But no offer came from the Crown. Instead there was further disappointment.

Some months before Carver submitted his petition to the Earl of Dartmouth, Robert Rogers, his reputation partially restored and his taste for daring exploits undiminished, had petitioned the Crown to authorize a new expedition through the American hinterland. Once more, he hoped to find the elusive Northwest Passage. His intention was to follow the Minnesota River, and then the Missouri. After a portage of some thirty miles, he would finally reach the "Great River Ourigan." Rogers argued that following that river would lead to the

Norman Gelb

fabled Straits of Annian on the Pacific coast. From there, the coast would be explored in search of the mouth of the waterway that he was convinced was the western end of the long-sought-after river passage through North America. To make his proposal more palatable to the Crown than his earlier one, Rogers submitted a requisition for a sum amounting to only a fraction of what he had previously requested.

Despite Carver's earlier disappointment with Rogers, when he learned of this new scheme, he grasped at the possibility of being included. It was a chance both to return to the American interior and finally to be usefully employed again. But Rogers was now viewed with considerable suspicion in London. Besides, the British authorities were even less inclined than before to sponsor new adventures in the American backcountry.

The situation had been growing increasingly tense in the colonies. The continuing presence of British garrisons in New York, Boston, and other cities angered the populace. A number of bloody clashes between Redcoats and Americans had taken place, the Boston Massacre in 1770 being the most famous. The Sons of Liberty had stepped up their harassment of local officials of the Crown who were entrusted with the implementation of British government laws and regulations. Committees of Correspondence, in which the seeds of independence sprouted, had been formed in American cities, towns, and villages. British goods were boycotted up and down the Atlantic coast. The First Continental Congress convened in 1774 in Philadelphia to provide a forum for concerted American resistance to the authority of the Crown.

Protests and organized resistance by the colonists had earlier compelled the British government to rescind or modify some of the taxes and restrictions it had imposed on the colonies. Edmund Burke and a number of other prominent English politicians urged the Crown to treat the colonies with sympathy and understanding. But angry mutterings about unwarranted appeasement of the unruly, ungrateful Americans had been growing in crescendo in London's corridors of power. From a British military commander in Boston had come word that open insurrection was increasingly probable. He advised that

"Leniency won't do now with the people here." At the same time, disturbing reports were received from Amsterdam and Hamburg of American ships secretly loading up with firearms.

The situation was plunging out of control. The Treasury in London was hard pressed to find additional resources to deal with the mounting security problems in the colonies as well as the likelihood that France would seize upon Britain's difficulties to seek advantage in the New World. It was precisely the wrong time for anyone to attempt to obtain authorization and funding for an expedition into the American hinterland. A new search for the Northwest Passage was hardly high on the Crown's list of priorities.

In any case, Rogers was soon behind bars in London for bankruptcy. He remained there until his brother raised funds to pay off his major creditors. Despairing of opportunities in London, he returned to America. The Revolution was now imminent. The Second Continental Congress was laying the groundwork. Minutemen clashed at Lexington, Massachusetts, with Redcoats sent to seize their weapons. Ethan Allen and the Green Mountain Boys seized the British fort at Ticonderoga. News of the Battle of Bunker Hill, in which Jonathan Carver's twenty-year-old son, Rufus, was among the Americans fighting the British, rallied the colonies to the cause of independence. George Washington journeyed to Boston to take command of the Continental Army. There could be no turning back.

Although on home ground once more, Robert Rogers was still at loose ends. He had neither funds nor employment. Unable to comprehend the ferment that was sweeping the colonies, he tried his hand at land speculation. Nothing came of it, but because of his movements in pursuit of land deals, he was suspected of being a British spy, and Washington had him arrested. Desperate and feeling persecuted, he escaped from imprisonment and sought renewed fame, glory, and the gratitude of the Crown by offering his services to the British Army in America. He recruited a detachment of American loyalists to fight the rebels.

The Queen's American Rangers, however, were not the sturdy backwoodsmen who had formed Rogers' elite unit of guerrilla fighters in the closing years of the French and Indian Wars. They made little impression either on the Continental Army or on their British superiors. They were soon defeated in battle and Rogers was relieved of his command. He soon felt obliged to flee back to England for safety. He died in debt and obscurity in a London boarding house in 1795.

The Publication of Carver's Journal

When the American Revolution erupted, Carver was sixty-five years old. To follow the lead Rogers had set and return without funds or prospects to an America in turmoil must have seemed unthinkable to him. He must also by then have despaired of receiving an appointment in the American hinterland or anywhere else from the Crown. Although his wife was still living back in Massachusetts, he had married again in London, to Mary Harris, the widow of a Royal Navy officer, with whom he had two children.

Carver received further small handouts from the Crown as a result of his successive petitions and pleadings. But his efforts to publish his journal remained frustrated. The fact that a growing number of Americans had been arriving in London with tales to tell probably worsened his chances. Loyal to the Crown when their compatriots were rising up in fury against it, they had abandoned their homeland to find sanctuary in the motherland. It is the only time in history that significant numbers of Americans have fled as refugees to another country.

Among those refugees were very prominent individuals, including former Massachusetts governor Thomas Hutchinson; William Smith, the former chief justice of the New York colony; Andrew Allen, who had been Pennsylvania's attorney general; former North Carolina governor John Randolph; and Isaac Low, who had been a member of the First Continental Congress. Tens of thousands of less eminent loyalists, unable to afford a transatlantic journey or to face the prospect of life so far from home, generally made instead for the safety of British lines in Canada, where they planted the seeds from which modern Canada subsequently developed.

Those who fled to England were not planning permanent exile. They intended to remain abroad only until His Majesty's Redcoats taught Washington's ragtag army proper manners. They intended to return when the king's writ once more ran supreme in the colonies. These refugees were initially welcomed by the English, who sympathized with their plight and appreciated their loyalty. Governor Hutchinson was even received by King George. But as the war dragged on, and as the loyalists increasingly petitioned the authorities for subsidies, pensions, and sinecures so that they might support themselves in their protracted exile, they began to overstay their welcome.

Some Britons sympathized with the American revolutionaries struggling against the odds in the name of liberty. The Earl of Chatham declared, "If I were an American as I am an Englishman, while a foreign troop was landed in my country I never would lay down my arms." But most English people condemned the rebellious Americans for "gnawing at the very entrails of Great Britain and spilling her best blood." For those bitter over the behavior of the colonists, the difference between rebels and loyalists began to blur. A more all-embracing anti-Americanism sank in.

Having arrived in London long before the rebellion had gathered momentum, Carver could not be numbered among those seeking sanctuary in England. His loyalties were not a factor in his presence there. It is not known what, if any, contact he had with his displaced compatriots. But their presence and the feelings they generated among the English could not have made life easier for another American suppliant in their midst.

By the time the colonies declared independence, Carver must have given up believing he would be awarded sufficient funds from the Crown to sustain himself and his English family or an appointment to an official position. His main hope was publication of an account of his travels.

It may have been apparent by then that his journal, as he had written it, was not a viable commercial proposition. Its text needed something more if it was to prove attractive in printed form to the

book buying public. It needed more adventure, more excitement.
Carver was prepared to provide both, as can be seen in the two ledger-sized volumes of his writings that were bequeathed to the British Museum by his friend, Sir Joseph Banks, after his death and that are still in the museum's manuscript collection. On a timeworn insert in the middle of one of those volumes is the statement, "The following is the same Journal put by the author into a form which he intends for Publication with several additions seem to have been made from Memory."

Some of the added material was anecdotal. Some of Carver's original observations were elaborated upon. But the journal in revised form apparently was still not considered publishable. To make it so, it was transformed into a book of more flowing narrative, with still more material inserted, some of it borrowed from other sources.

As in Boston a decade earlier, Carver appears to have advertised the new literary product he wished to sell. He was again troubled by printing costs. In a letter to Banks in 1778, he complained that "tho' I have been favoured with a number of subscribers, they are not more than sufficient to pay one third of the expences of printing."

Nevertheless, the book, titled *Travels Through the Interior Parts of North America In the Years 1766, 1767, and 1768*, was published a few months later. The journal had been transformed. Some of its contents had been omitted but much was added. The story focused in greater depth on the terrain of "the interior" and especially on the people who lived there. The account was now an eminently readable and often thoughtful work.

Carver took many liberties with the truth. Some of his descriptions of Indian life were unwarranted generalizations. He exaggerated his own role in the expedition, making no reference to his having been commissioned by Rogers merely to draw maps and make observations. The roles played by Rogers, Tute, and Goddard were greatly downplayed in his account so that he emerged very much the central figure in this search for the Northwest Passage. The impression given was that he had not been motivated by any thought of monetary reward for himself, but that if others had the vision and found the means to exploit the riches of the territory he had explored, they would earn "Emoluments beyond their most sanguine expectations."

An editor may have contributed significantly to transforming Carver's writings into the polished product the book became. In his revised journal, Carver included a message to an unnamed "Reviser" on how the contents might be made easier for readers to understand and welcoming any embellishment that would "give better sence" to his account. Although no written credit was given, Alexander Bicknell, an English contemporary of Carver and a prolific author of no great accomplishment, later claimed to be editor of the book, and his claim does not appear to have been disputed by any of Carver's patrons or friends. Such uncredited editing of writings for publication was not uncommon.

On publication, *Travels* was well received by the London critics. One magazine included long passages that testified to continuing British interest in the American backcountry and its inhabitants despite the rambunctiousness of the colonial revolutionaries. Carver was described in one review as "a judicious and faithful observer." But publication of the book in 1778 did not greatly serve to improve his fortunes. Neither did a second edition published the following year, nor did his *Treatise On the Culture of the Tobacco Plant*, also published in London in 1779.

So desperate were Carver's circumstances that to support himself and his family he was compelled to take work as a lottery clerk. He appears also to have worked as a map maker for a London publisher. A different book of travels, *The New Universal Traveller, Containing a Full and Distinct Account of All the Empires, Kingdoms and States in the Known World*, was published under his name in 1779. But it was probably compiled by others, with Carver receiving some payment for the use of his name, which had begun to attract critical attention in London's literary world. His British wife later denied it was his work.

Carver had finally achieved recognition for his exertions in the American wilderness. But monetary reward continued to escape him, and he died in poverty in London on January 31, 1780. A notice in

Gentleman's Magazine of March that year was "sorry to inform our readers that we are well assured Capt. Carver . . . died absolutely and strictly starved, leaving a wife and two small children." The magazine noted that many copies of his book had been "disposed of," but despite its "great merit," it had been unable to "procure him a competent provision." Friends and literary figures organized a fund to help support Carver's London family.

Another edition of *Travels* appeared a year after Carver's death and was again well received. It included a biographical sketch of the author by Dr. John Coakley Lettsom, a founder of the Medical Society of London. In it, Lettsom offered the following description:

> In size, Captain Carver was rather above middle stature, and of a firm muscular texture; his features expressed a firmness of mind and boldness of resolution; and he retained a florid complexion to his latest moments. In conversation he was social and affable, where he was familiar; but his extreme diffidence and modesty kept him in general reserved in company. In his familiar epistles, he commanded an easy and agreeable manner of writing; and some pieces of his poetry, which have been communicated to me, afford proofs of his lively imagination.

Lettsom's biographical sketch of Carver contained several errors. Lettsom described him as having been born in 1732, by which time Carver was already twenty-two years old. People generally deteriorated physically much more quickly in those days than they do now, and it appears that Lettsom met Carver only shortly before he died. Unless Carver was in remarkably robust physical condition, it is extraordinary that a doctor would have been fooled into believing that this septuagenarian was only forty-eight years old. Lettsom also mistakenly claimed that Carver was the grandson of an officer in King William's army and wrongly identified his place of birth. It would appear that Carver deliberately misinformed the doctor about his personal history. He may have felt it advisable to misrepresent his age and antecedents in order to establish the impression he desired among those in England whose favor he sought and from whom he sought employment.

The first American edition of the book was published in the newly independent United States in Philadelphia in 1784. Before the turn of the nineteenth century, several further editions of the book were published in America and elsewhere, testifying to its popularity. Accounts by others of their journeys through the American hinterland had previously been written, notably by French explorers, but none had aroused as much interest or widespread acclaim as Carver's. His was the first truly popular American travel book.

But it was considered more than that. Other explorers, map makers, and writers studied it for useful information. A London journal claimed in 1815 that in giving an account of their historic exploration of the American West four decades after Carver's trek, Meriwether Lewis and William Clark had made free use of *Travels* without crediting its author and suggested that "it would not have misbecome [them] if they had bestowed upon their able and enterprizing forerunner, the commendation which he anticipated and desired."

That was unfair comment, as Lewis and Clark traversed far wider regions than Carver had. But it did indicate the esteem in which the earlier explorer was held at the time. Others who penetrated uncharted western regions, Zebulon Montgomery Pike—the explorer for whom Pikes Peak was named—among them, indicated their familiarity with Carver's work.

Carver's Legacy

During the nineteenth century, as increasing numbers of explorers ventured westward and recorded their observations, and as others followed to settle in the region Carver had charted, *Travels* was superseded by more up-to-date accounts. Interest in the book declined, except among historians, some of whom expressed doubts about the veracity of Carver's account. Among them was Robert Greenhow, who charged in 1844 that the book "was written, or rather made up" in London at the suggestion of Carver's friends "and printed for the purpose of relieving the wants of the author, who, however, died there, in misery." Edward Gaylord Bourne, another

46

historian, suggested in 1906 that the book was nothing more than a compilation of musings and borrowings from other explorers. Bourne maintained that Carver had been only an "unlettered Connecticut shoemaker," incapable either of undertaking a major exploratory expedition or of writing intelligently about it.

Those claims were baseless, and they were effectively refuted by John Thomas Lee in 1909. Lee located the advertisement Carver had placed in the *Boston Chronicle* in 1768 at the conclusion of his travels, when he was seeking subscribers to help finance publication of his journal in Massachusetts before he left for England. In another 1768 edition of that newspaper, Lee found the long, intelligent, informative, well-composed letter Carver had written to his wife from Michilimackinac during the winter of 1767 at the conclusion of his trek. There could be no denying that the letter contained some of the observations and stories that were later to be contained and expanded upon in the book.

Lee conceded that Bourne was correct in saying that Carver's account contained material plagiarized from the French explorers Father Louis Hennepin, Baron Louis-Armand de Lahontan, and Pierre de Charlevoix, and also from the American explorer James Adair. Carver may have met Adair in London, where they may have exchanged stories about their experiences and observations. But such "borrowings" were not uncommon at the time and occur occasionally even today in works that are otherwise commendable. Charges that the book was either a total fabrication or the work of another hand were conclusively refuted by the discovery of Carver's original journal, and alterations he made to it, both in Carver's handwriting, in the British Museum.

By then another controversy over the book had been effectively put to rest. The introduction that Dr. Lettsom wrote to the third edition contained a claim that two Sioux chiefs had granted Carver a large tract of land, amounting to some 12,000 square miles of the Midwest. It included most of the northwestern quarter of what is now Wisconsin. This bestowal was supposedly a reward for his having mediated a dispute between the Sioux and the Chippewa, and for having "conciliated their attachment and friendship." Lettsom claimed to have the deed in his possession and quoted it in the introduction:

> To Jonathan Carver, a chief under the most mighty and potent George the Third, King of the English and other nations, the fame of whose courageous warriors have reached our ears, and has been more fully told us by our good brother Jonathan aforesaid, whom we rejoice to see come among us, and bring us good news from his country. We, chiefs of the Naudowissies, who have hereto set our seals, do by these presents for ourselves and heirs for ever, in return for many presents, and other good services done by the said Jonathan to ourselves and allies, give, grant, and convey to him the said Jonathan, and to his heirs and assigns for ever, the whole of a certain tract of territory of land, bounded as follows: (viz.) from the fall of St. Anthony, running on the east banks of the Mississippi, nearly south-east, as far as the south end of Lake Pepin, where the Chipeway river joins the Mississippi, and from thence eastward five days travel, accounting twenty English miles per day, and from thence north six days travel, at twenty English miles per day, and from then again to the fall of St. Anthony, on a direct straight line. We do for ourselves, heirs, and assigns, for ever, give unto the said Jonathan, his heirs and assigns, for ever, all the said lands, with all the trees, rocks, and rivers therein, reserving for ourselves and heirs the sole liberty of hunting and fishing on land not planted or improved by the said Jonathan, his heirs and assigns, to which we have affixed our respective seals, at the great cave, [located within the city limits of present day St. Paul] May the first, one thousand seven hundred and sixty-seven.

The Sioux chiefs awarding this prize were identified by Lettsom as Hawnopawjatin and Otohtongoomlisheaw, both of whom were said to have affixed their totem marks.

The actual deed was never found. Some such document probably existed and may well have been genuine. Lettsom was a reputable figure who had nothing to gain from fabricating it or publishing its contents. In a letter to a friend, he said he had been shown the deed by Carver's British widow, "a paper of half a sheet with two marks said to be those of Indian chiefs at the foot of a grant of Land." Carver himself made no mention of it in his journal or in the body of his book, nor did he make any claim to the Crown on the basis of it. He may have accepted that the deed, if it was genuine and not something he himself had concocted, was little more than a curiosity, carrying no legal weight. Lettsom searched for the document after Mary Carver died some years later, but he was unable to find it and could only conclude that it was no longer in existence.

But in 1804, Samuel Harrison, an Englishman then living in Chittendon, Vermont, wrote about the deed to Samuel Peters, an Anglican minister, formerly of Hebron, Connecticut, who, as a loyalist, had fled for refuge to England shortly before the outbreak of the Revolution and who was still living there. Harrison was distantly related by marriage to one of Jonathan Carver's American grand-daughters. He wanted Peters to help him discover whether any British claimants to the Carver legacy existed.

Harrison subsequently petitioned Congress on behalf of Carver's heirs in the United States for ratification of the deed. Peters meantime had begun taking a personal interest in the matter. He returned to America and spent his remaining years actively engaged in trying to prove the deed's validity and seeking to profit from it. In 1806, claiming to represent Carver's heirs, he sought an appointment with President Thomas Jefferson to review the matter. Referred to a committee of the Senate, he claimed that he had been with Lettsom at Carver's deathbed and that Carver had begged the two of them to win ratification of the land grant "for the benefit of his children and country." In view of his not having troubled with the matter until contacted by Harrison two years earlier, that seemed unlikely. But Peters claimed he was advised by the Senate committee that the claim would be ratified if it was confirmed by existing Sioux chiefs.

Having made an agreement with Carver's American descendants, Peters then dispatched an agent to seek ratification of the deed by the Sioux. That agent was taken prisoner by an Indian war party and was not released for several years. Two other men Peters sent were also prevented by unsettled conditions from completing their missions.

By 1812, Peters was claiming to be owner of the land in question and was attempting to sell bits of it to anyone who could pay cash.

Several of Carver's heirs were attempting to do the same. Financial backers and land companies were soon involved. In 1817, two grandsons of Jonathan Carver traveled up the Mississippi from Prairie du Chien but failed to receive Sioux confirmation of the deed. That same year, Peters himself, although now eighty-three years old, set off, accompanied by a small party, for the Falls of St. Anthony with the same objective. But the army commander at Fort Crawford, which had now been established at Prairie du Chien, said he had no authority to permit Peters to enter Indian territory, and he was forced to turn back after spending the winter there. He continued to press for legal confirmation of the Indian land grant. But in 1825, a congressional committee ruled conclusively that the claim had no legitimate basis.

In the years that followed, gullible individuals continued to be induced to part with money for a share of the "Carver grant" territory. Rumors circulated from time to time that the missing deed had been found, and further claimants appeared regularly. As late as 1921, in a history of Minnesota published by the Minnesota Historical Society, William Watt Folwell observed, "If the present governor of Minnesota has not been addressed by some person believing himself a rightful beneficiary of the claim, his experience is exceptional."

The interior region of America through which Jonathan Carver trekked, and about which he left a detailed record, was a place of fascination and splendor, and Carver was a visionary. He saw not only the awesome wilderness that the interior of America once was—its magnificent landscapes, profusion of wildlife, and endless assortment of plant life; he also envisioned a domain where "mighty kingdoms" would emerge, with "stately palaces and solemn temples, with gilded spires reaching the skies."

But the lasting significance and fascination of Carver's work undoubtedly resides in the treasure trove of his accounts of American Indian life. The observations Carver made and the conclusions he drew about the American Indians he met and lived among inevitably were influenced by the values of his time and background. But unlike most of his contemporaries, he recognized their distinctive humanity, the intricacies of their cultures, and the richness of the environment in which they lived, and he wrote about them without gloss or bias.

A Note on This Edition

This edited version of *Jonathan Carver's Travels Through the Interior Parts of North America* is based on the edition published in London in 1781. That edition, however, included much material that was not in Carver's original manuscript journals, material that it seems was added to address subjects of popular interest and perhaps merely to bulk out the book.

One long passage, for example, describes the theories of various writers of that and earlier periods concerning the geographic and ethnic origins of the American Indians. Most of this was baseless speculation and is of little value now that ethnologists, archaeologists, and others have provided more substantial insights into the migrations of the first Americans. Another sizable addition is a detailed account of insect life, snakes, birds, and flora of the region that Carver explored, information that similarly has been largely superseded by later studies and that offers little of enduring value.

These and similar sections and passages, which are not germane to Carver's expedition and add little to our understanding, have not been included in this edition, the purpose of which is to recapture the unique first-hand impression of the people Jonathan Carver encountered on his travels into the American interior and the setting in which he beheld them.

For ease of reading, ellipses have not been used to indicate areas of excision. Archaic or British spellings and usages have been left as they were, except where they might lead to misunderstanding or confusion. In places, punctuation has been made to conform to current usage for the same reason.

Jonathan Carver's
Travels Through America

Part One

JONATHAN CARVER'S TRAVELS

Travels Through the Interior Parts of North America

BY JONATHAN CARVER, *Esquire*

N O SOONER was the late War with France concluded, and Peace established by the Treaty of Versailles in the year 1763, than I began to consider—having rendered my country some services during the war—how I might continue to be still serviceable and contribute, as much as lay in my power, to make that vast acquisition of territory gained by Great Britain in North America advantageous to it. It appeared to me indispensably needful, that Government should be acquainted in the first place with the true state of the dominions they were now become possessed of.

To this purpose, I determined, as the next proof of my zeal, to explore the most unknown parts of them and to spare no trouble or expence in acquiring a knowledge that promised to be so useful to my countrymen. I knew that many obstructions would arise to my scheme from the want of good Maps and Charts; for the French, whilst they retained their power in North America, had taken every artful method to keep all other nations, particularly the English, in ignorance of the concerns of the interior parts of it. To accomplish this design with the greater certainty, they had published inaccurate maps and false accounts, calling the different nations of the Indians by nicknames they had given them and not by those really appertaining to them. Whether the intention of the French in doing this was to prevent those nations from being discovered and traded with, or to conceal their discourse when they talked to each other of the Indian concerns in their presence, I will not determine. But whatsoever was the cause from which it arose, it tended to mislead.

It cannot be denied but that some maps have been published by the French with an appearance of accuracy. But these are of so small a size and drawn on so minute a scale, that they are nearly inexplicable. The sources of the Mississippi, I can assert from my own experience, are greatly misplaced; for when I had explored them, and compared their situation with the French Charts, I found them very erroneously represented and am satisfied that these were only copied from the rude sketches of the Indians.

These difficulties, however, were not sufficient to deter me from the undertaking, and I made preparations for setting out. What I chiefly had in view, after gaining a knowledge of the Manners, Customs, Languages, Soil, and natural Productions of the different [Indian] nations that inhabit the back of the Mississippi, was to ascertain the Breadth of that vast continent which extends from the Atlantic to the Pacific Ocean, in its broadest part between 43 and 46 Degrees Northern Latitude. Had I been able to accomplish this, I intended to have proposed to Government to establish a Post in some of those parts.

This I am convinced would greatly facilitate the discovery of a Northwest Passage, or a communication between Hudson's Bay and the Pacific Ocean, an event so desirable, and which has been so often sought for, but without success. Besides this important end, a settlement on that extremity of America would answer many good purposes, and repay every expence the establishment of it might occasion. For it would not only disclose new sources of trade, and promote many useful discoveries, but open a passage for conveying intelligence to China and the English settlements in the East Indies with greater expedition than a tedious voyage by the Cape of Good Hope or the Straits of Magellan will allow of.

How far the advantages arising from such an enterprize may extend can only be ascertained by the favourable concurrence of future events. But that the completion of the scheme I have the honour of first planning and attempting will some time or other be effected, I have no doubt. From the unhappy divisions that at present subsist between Great Britain and America, it will probably be some years before the attempt is repeated. But whenever it is, and the execution of it carried on with propriety, those who are so fortunate as to succeed will reap, exclusive of the national advantages that must ensue, Emoluments beyond their most sanguine expectations. And whilst their spirits are elated by their success, perhaps they may bestow some commendations and blessings on the person that first pointed out to them the way. These, though but a shadowy recompence for all my toil, I shall receive with pleasure.

To what power or authority this new world will become dependent, after it has arisen from its present uncultivated state, time alone can discover. But as the seat of Empire from time immemorial has been gradually progressive towards the West, there is no doubt that at some future period, mighty kingdoms will emerge from these wildernesses and stately palaces and solemn temples with gilded spires reaching the skies will supplant the Indian huts whose only decorations are the barbarous trophies of their vanquished enemies.

The plan I had laid down for penetrating to the Pacific Ocean, proved abortive but it is necessary to add that this proceeded not from its impracticability (for the farther I went the more convinced I was that it could certainly be accomplished) but from unforeseen disappointments. However, I proceeded so far that I was able to make such discoveries as will be useful in any future attempt, and prove a good foundation for some more fortunate Successor to build upon. These I shall now lay before the Public in the following pages and am satisfied that the greatest part of them have never been published by any person that has hitherto treated of the interior Nations of the Indians; particularly, the account I give of the Naudowessies, and the situation of the Heads of the four great rivers that take their rise within a few leagues of each other, nearly about the center of this great continent— The River Bourbon, which empties itself into Hudson's Bay; the Waters of Saint Lawrence; the Mississippi; and the River Oregon, or the River of the West, that falls into the Pacific Ocean at the Straits of Annian.

The impediments that occasioned my returning before I had accomplished my purposes were these. On my arrival at Michilimackinac, the remotest English post, in September 1766, I applied to Mr. Rogers, who was then governor of it, to furnish me with a proper assortment of goods, as presents for the Indians who inhabit the track I intended to pursue. He did this only in part but promised to supply me with such as were necessary when I reached the Falls of Saint Anthony. I afterwards learned that the governor fulfilled his promise in ordering the goods to be delivered to me, but those to whose care he intrusted them, instead of conforming to his orders, disposed of them elsewhere.

Disappointed in my expectations from this quarter, I thought it necessary to return to La Prairie le Chien for it was impossible to proceed any farther without presents to ensure me a favourable reception. This I did in the beginning of the year 1767, and finding my progress to the Westward thus retarded, I determined to direct my course Northward. I took this step with a view to meeting, at the grand Portage on the North-west side of Lake Superior, the traders that usually come about this season from Michilimackinac. Of these I intended to purchase goods, and then to pursue my journey from that quarter by way of the lakes de Pluye, Dubois, and Ounipique to the Heads of the river of the West, which falls into the Straits of Annian, the termination of my intended progress.

I accomplished the former part of my design and reached Lake Superior in proper time. But unluckily the traders I met there acquainted me that they had no goods to spare; those they had with them being barely sufficient to answer their own demands in these remote parts. Thus disappointed a second time, I found myself obliged to return to the place from whence I began my expedition, which I did after continuing some months on the North and East borders of Lake Superior, and exploring the Bays and Rivers that empty themselves into this large body of water.

As it may be expected that I should lay before the Public the reasons that these discoveries, of so much importance to every one who has any connections with America, have not been imparted to them before notwithstanding they were made upwards of ten years ago, I will give them to the world in a plain and candid manner, and without mingling with them any complaints on account of the ill treatment I have received.

On my arrival in England, I presented a petition to his Majesty in council, praying for a reimbursement of those sums I had expended in the service of government. This was referred to the Lords Commissioners of Trade and Plantations. Their Lordships from the tenor of it thought the intelligence I could give of so much importance to the nation that they ordered me to appear before the Board. This message I obeyed, and underwent a long examination, much I believe to the satisfaction of every Lord present.

When it was finished, I requested to know what I should do with my papers. Without hesitation the first Lord replied that I might publish them whenever I pleased. In consequence of this permission, I disposed of them to a bookseller. But when they were nearly ready for the press, an order was issued from the council board requiring me to deliver, without delay, into the Plantation Office, all my Charts and Journals, with every paper relative to the discoveries I had made.

In order to obey this command, I was obliged to re-purchase them from the bookseller, at a very great expence, and deliver them up. This fresh disbursement I endeavoured to get annexed to the account I had already delivered in. But the request was denied me, notwithstanding I had only acted, in the disposal of my papers, conformably to the permission I had received from the Board of Trade. This loss, which amounted to a very considerable sum, I was obliged to bear, and to rest satisfied with an indemnification for my other expences.

Thus situated, my only expectations are from the favour of a generous Public to whom I shall now communicate my Plans, Journals and Observations, of which I luckily kept copies when I delivered the originals into the Plantation Office. And this I do the more readily as I hear they are mislaid and there is no probability of their ever being published.

To those who are interested in the concerns of the interior parts of North America, from the contiguity of their possessions or commercial engagements, they will be extremely useful and fully repay the sum at which they are purchased. To those who from a laudable curiosity wish to be acquainted with the manners and customs of every inhabitant of this globe, the accounts here given of the various nations that inhabit so vast a track of it, a country hitherto almost unexplored, will furnish an ample fund of amusement and gratify their most curious expectations.

To make the following Work as comprehensible and entertaining as possible, I shall first give my Readers an account of the route I pursued over this immense continent and as I pass on, describe the number of Inhabitants, the situation of the Rivers and Lakes, and the productions of the country. Having done this, I shall treat, in distinct Chapters, of the Manners, Customs, and Languages of the Indians.

And here it is necessary to bespeak the candour of the learned part of my Readers in the perusal of it, as it is the production of a person unused, from opposite avocations, to literary pursuits. He therefore begs they would not examine it with too critical an eye; especially when he assures them that his attention has been more employed on giving a just description of a country that promises in some future period to be an inexhaustible source of riches to that people who shall be so fortunate as to possess it, than on the style or composition; and more careful to render his language intelligible and explicit than smooth and florid.

IN JUNE 1766, I set out from Boston, and proceeded by way of Albany and Niagara to Michilimackinac, a Fort situated between the Lakes Huron and Michigan and distant from Boston 1300 miles. This being the uttermost of our factories* towards the north-west, I considered it as the most convenient place from whence I could begin my intended progress, and enter at once into the regions I designed to explore.

Referring my Readers to the publications already extant for an Account of those Parts of North America that, from lying adjacent to the Back-Settlements, have been frequently described, I shall confine myself to a Description of the more interior parts of it which, having been but seldom visited, are consequently but little known. In doing this, I shall in no instance exceed the bounds of truth, or have recourse to those useless and extravagent exaggerations too often made use of by travellers to excite the curiosity of the public or to increase their own importance. Nor shall I insert any observations but such as I have made myself or, from the credibility of those by whom they were related, am enabled to vouch for their authenticity.

Michilimackinac, from whence I began my travels, is a Fort composed of a strong stockade and is usually defended by a garrison of one hundred men. It contains about thirty houses, one of which belongs to the governor and another to the commissary. Several traders also dwell within its fortifications who find it a convenient situation to traffic with the neighbouring nations. Michilimackinac, in the language of the Chipeway Indians, signifies a Tortoise and the place is supposed to receive its name from the Island lying about six

* Trading settlements maintained by and for factors (agents of companies based elsewhere).

or seven miles to the north-east, within sight of the Fort, which has the appearance of that animal.

During the Indian war that followed soon after the Conquest of Canada in the year 1763, and which was carried on by an army of confederate nations composed of the Hurons, Miamis, Chipeways, Ottowaws, Pontowattimies, Misissauges, and some other tribes, under the direction of Pontiac, a celebrated Indian warrior who had always been in the French interest, it was taken by surprise in the following manner: The Indians having settled their plan, drew near the Fort and began a game of ball, a pastime much used among them and not unlike tennis. In the height of their game, at which some of the English officers, not suspecting any deceit, stood looking, they struck the ball as if by accident over the stockade. This they repeated two or three times to make the deception more complete till at length, having by this means lulled every suspicion of the centry at the south gate, a party rushed by him. The rest soon following, they took possession of the Fort without meeting with any opposition. Having accomplished their design, the Indians had the humanity to spare the lives of the greatest part of the garrison and traders, but they made them all prisoners and carried them off. However some time after, they took them to Montreal where they were redeemed at a good price. The Fort also was given up again to the English at the peace made with Pontiac by the commander of Detroit the year following.

Having here made the necessary dispositions for pursuing my travels, and obtained a credit from Mr. Rogers, the governor, on some English and Canadian traders who were going to trade on the Mississippi, and received also from him a promise of a fresh supply of goods when I reached the Falls of Saint Anthony, I left the Fort on the 3d of September in company with these traders. It was agreed that they should furnish me with such goods as I might want for presents to the Indian chiefs during my continuance with them. But when I arrived at the extent of their route, I was to find other guides and to depend on the goods the governor had promised to supply me with.

We accordingly set out together and on the 18th arrived at Fort La Bay. This Fort is situated on the southern extremity of a Bay in Lake

Michigan, termed by the French the Bay of Puants but which, since the English have gained possession of all the settlements on this part of the Continent, is called by them the Green Bay. The reason of its being thus denominated is from its appearance, for on leaving Michilimackinac in the spring season, though the trees there have not even put forth their buds, yet you find the country around La Bay, notwithstanding the passage has not exceeded fourteen days, covered with the finest verdure and vegetation as forward as it could be were it summer.

This Fort also is only surrounded by a stockade and, being much decayed, is scarcely defensible against small arms. It was built by the French for the protection of their trade some time before they were forced to relinquish it. When Canada and its dependencies were surrendered to the English, it was immediately garrisoned with an officer and thirty men. These were made prisoners by the Menomonies soon after the surprise of Michilimackinac and the Fort has neither been garrisoned or kept in repair since.

The Bay is about ninety miles long but differs much in its breadth; being in some places only fifteen miles, in others from twenty to thirty. It lies nearly from north-east to south-east. At the entrance of it from the Lake are a string of islands extending from north to south, called the Grand Traverse. These are about thirty miles in length and serve to facilitate the passage of canoes as they shelter from the winds, which sometimes come with violence across the Lake. On the side that lies to the south-east is the nearest and best navigation.

The islands of the Grand Traverse are mostly small and rocky. Many of the rocks are of an amazing size and appear as if they had been fashioned by the hands of artists. On the largest and best of these islands stand a town of the Ottowaws, at which I found one of the most considerable chiefs of that nation who received me with every honour he could possibly show to a stranger. But what appeared extremely singular to me at the time, and must do to every person unacquainted with the customs of the Indians, was the reception I met with on landing.

As our canoes approached the shore and had reached within about threescore rods of it, the Indians began a feu-de-joy, in which they fired their pieces loaded with balls, but at the same time they took care to discharge them in such a manner as to fly a few yards above our heads. During this they ran from one tree or stump to another, shouting and behaving as if they were in the heat of battle. At first I was greatly surprized and was on the point of ordering my attendants to return their fire, concluding that their intentions were hostile. But being undeceived by some of the traders, who informed me that this was their usual method of receiving the chiefs of other nations, I considered it in its true light, and was pleased with the respect thus paid me.

I remained here one night. Among the presents I made the chiefs were some spirituous liquors, with which they made themselves merry, and all joined in a dance that lasted the greatest part of the night. In the morning when I departed, the chief attended me to the shore and, as soon as I had embarked, offered up, in an audible voice and with great solemnity, a fervent prayer in my behalf. He prayed that the Great Spirit would favour me with a prosperous voyage, that he would give me an unclouded sky and smooth waters by day, and that I might lie down by night on a beaver blanket, enjoying uninterrupted sleep and pleasant dreams, and also that I might find continual protection under the great pipe of peace. In this manner he continued his petitions till I could no longer hear them.

I must here observe that, notwithstanding the inhabitants of Europe are apt to entertain horrid ideas of the ferocity of these savages, as they are termed, I received from every tribe of them in the interior parts the most hospitable and courteous treatment and am convinced that till they are contaminated by the example and spirituous liquors of their more refined neighbours, they retain this friendly and inoffensive conduct towards strangers. Their inveteracy and cruelty to their enemies I acknowledge to be a great abatement of the favourable opinion I would wish to entertain. But this failing is hereditary of them, and having received the sanction of immemorial custom, has taken too deep root in their minds to be ever extirpated.

Among this people I ate of a very uncommon kind of bread. The

Indians, in general, use but little of this nutritious food. Whilst their corn is in the milk, as they term it, that is just before it begins to ripen, they slice off the kernels from the cob to which they grow and knead them into a paste. This they are enabled to do, without the addition of any liquid, by the milk that flows from them. When it is effected, they parcel it out into cakes and, inclosing them in leaves of the basswood tree, place them in hot embers where they are soon baked. And better flavoured bread I never ate in any country.

This place is only a small village containing about twenty-five houses and sixty or seventy warriors. I found nothing there worthy of further remark.

The land on the south-east side of the Green Bay is but very indifferent, being overspread with a heavy growth of hemlock, pine, spruce and fir trees. The communication between Lake Michigan and the Green Bay has been reported by some to be impracticable for the passage of any vessels larger than canoes or boats on account of the shoals that lie between the islands in the Grand Traverse. But on sounding it, I found sufficient depth for a vessel of sixty tons, and the breadth proportionable.

The land adjoining to the bottom of this Bay is very fertile, the country in general level, and the perspective view is pleasing and extensive.

A few families live in the Fort which lies on the west-side of the Fox River, and opposite to it, on the east-side of its entrance, are some French settlers who cultivate the land and appear to live very comfortably.

The Green Bay or Bay of Puants is one of those places to which the French have given nicknames. It is termed by the inhabitants of its coasts the Menomonie Bay. But why the French have denominated it the Puant or Stinking Bay I know not. The reason they themselves give for it is that it was not with a view to mislead strangers, but that by adopting this method they could converse with each other concerning the Indians in their presence without being understood by them.

Lake Michigan, of which the Green Bay is part, is divided on the northeast from Lake Huron by the Straits of Michilimackinac and is situated between forty-two and forty-six degrees of latitude and between eighty-four and eighty-seven degrees of west longitude. Its greatest length is two hundred and eighty miles, its breadth about forty, and its circumference nearly six hundred. There is a remarkable string of small islands beginning over against Askin's Farm, and running about thirty miles southwest into the Lake. These are called the Beaver Islands. Their situation is very pleasant but the soil is bare. However they afford a beautiful prospect.

On the north-west parts of this Lake the waters branch out into two bays. That which lies towards the north is the Bay of Noquets, and the other the Green Bay just described.

The waters of this as well as the other great Lakes are clear and wholesome and of sufficient depth for the navigation of large ships. Half the space of the country that lies to the east, and extends to Lake Huron, belongs to the Ottowaw Indians. The line that divides their territories from the Chipeways, runs nearly north and south, and reaches almost from the southern extremity of this Lake, across the high lands, to Michilimackinac, through the center of which it passes. So that when these two tribes happen to meet at the factory, they each encamp on their own dominions, at a few yards distance from the stockade.

The country adjacent either to the east or west side of the lake is composed but of an indifferent soil, except where small brooks or rivers empty themselves into it on the banks of these it is extremely fertile. Near the borders of the Lake grow a great number of sand cherries, which are not less remarkable for their manner of growth than for their excellent flavour. They grow upon a small shrub not more than four feet high, the boughs of which are so loaded that they lie in clusters on the sand. As they grow only on the sand, the warmth of which probably contributes to bring them to such perfection, they are called by the French, cherries de sable or sand cherries. The size of them does not exceed that of a small musket ball, but they are reckoned superior to any other sort for the purpose of steeping in spirits. There also grow around the Lake gooseberries, black currants, and an abundance of juniper, bearing great quantities of berries of the finest sort.

Sumack likewise grows here in great plenty, the leaf of which, gathered at Michaelmas when it turns red, is much esteemed by the natives. They mix about an equal quantity of it with their tobacco which causes it to smoke pleasantly. Near this Lake, and indeed about all the great lakes, is found a kind of willow, termed by the French, bois rouge, in English red wood. Its bark, when only of one year's growth, is of a fine scarlet colour, and appears very beautiful; but as it grows older, it changes into a mixture of grey and red. The stalks of this shrub grow many of them together and rise to the height of six or eight feet, the largest not exceeding an inch diameter.

The bark being scraped from the sticks and dried and powdered is also mixed by the Indians with their tobacco and is held by them in the highest estimation for their winter smoking. A weed that grows near the great lakes, in rocky places, they use in the summer season. It is called by the Indians Segockimac and creeps like a vine on the ground, sometimes extending to eight or ten feet and bearing a leaf about the size of a silver penny, nearly round. It is of the substance and colour of the laurel and is, like the tree it resembles, an evergreen. These leaves, dried and powdered, they likewise mix with their tobacco and, as said before, smoke it only during the summer. By these three succedaneums, the pipes of the Indians are well supplied through every season of the year and as they are great smokers, they are very careful in properly gathering and preparing them.

On the 20th of September, I left the Green Bay and proceeded up Fox River, still in company with the traders and some Indians. On the 25th, I arrived at the great town of the Winnebagoes, situated on a small island just as you enter the east end of Lake Winnebago. Here the queen who presided over this tribe instead of a Sachem received me with great civility and entertained me in a very distinguished manner during the four days I continued with her.

The day after my arrival I held a council with the chiefs, of whom I asked permission to pass through their country on my way to more

69

remote nations on business of importance. This was readily granted me, the request being esteemed by them a great compliment paid to their tribe. The queen sat in the council, but only asked a few questions or gave some trifling directions in matters relative to the state, for women are never allowed to sit in their councils, except they happen to be invested with the supreme authority, and then it is not customary for them to make formal speeches as the chiefs do. She was a very ancient woman, small in stature and not much distinguished by her dress from several young women that attended her. These, her attendants, seemed greatly pleased whenever I showed any tokens of respect to their queen, particularly when I saluted her, which I frequently did to acquire her favour. On these occasions the good lady endeavoured to assume a juvenile gaity, and by her smiles showed she was equally pleased with the attention I paid her.

The time I tarried here, I employed in making the best observations possible on the country, and in collecting the most certain intelligence I could of the origin, language, and customs of this people. From these enquiries I have reason to conclude that the Winnebagoes originally resided in some of the provinces belonging to New Mexico; and being driven from their native country, either by intestine divisions or by the extension of the Spanish conquests, they took refuge in these more northern parts about a century ago.

My reasons for adopting this supposition are, first from their unalienable attachment to the Naudowessie Indians (who, they say, gave them the earliest succour during their emigration) notwithstanding their present residence is more than six hundred miles from that people. Secondly, that their dialect totally differs from every other Indian nation yet discovered; it being a very uncouth gutteral jargon which none of their neighbours will attempt to learn. They converse with other nations in the Chipeway tongue, which is the prevailing language throughout all the tribes, from the Mohawks of Canada to those who inhabit the borders of the Mississippi, and from the Hurons and Illinois to such as dwell near Hudson's Bay.

Thirdly, from their inveterate hatred of the Spaniards. Some of them informed me that they had made many excursions to the southwest which took several moons. An elderly chief more particularly acquainted me that about forty-six winters ago, he marched at the head of fifty warriors towards the south-west for three moons. That during this expedition, whilst they were crossing a plain, they discovered a body of men on horseback who belong to the Black People, for so they call the Spaniards. As soon as they perceived them, they proceeded with caution and concealed themselves till night came on, when they drew so near as to be able to discern the number and situation of their enemies.

Finding they were not able to cope with so great a superiority by day-light, they waited till they had retired to rest, when they rushed upon them and, after having killed the greatest part of the men, took eighty horses loaded with what they termed white stone. This I suppose to have been silver, as he told me the horses were shod with it and that their bridles were ornamented with the same. When they had satiated their revenge, they carried off their spoil and being got so far as to be out of the reach of the Spaniards that had escaped their fury, they left the useless and ponderous burthen with which the horses were loaded in the woods and mounting themselves, returned to their friends. The party they had thus defeated I concluded to be the caravan that annually conveys to Mexico the silver which the Spaniards find in great quantities on the mountains lying near the heads of the Colorado River and the plains where the attack was made.

The Winnebagoes can raise about two hundred warriors. Their town contains about fifty houses which are strongly built with palisades, and the island on which it is situated nearly fifty acres. It lies thirty-five miles, reckoning according to the course of the river, from the Green Bay.

The River, for about four or five miles from the Bay, has a gentle current. After that space, till you arrive at the Winnebago Lake, it is full of rocks and very rapid. At many places we were obliged to land our canoes, and carry them a considerable way. The land adjacent to the Lake is very fertile, abounding with grapes, plums, and other fruits, which grow spontaneously. The Winnebagoes raise on it a great quantity of Indian corn, beans, pumpkins, squash, and water melons, with some tobacco. The Lake itself abounds with fish, and in the fall of the year, with geese, ducks, and teal. The latter, which resort to it in great numbers, are remarkably good and extremely fat and are much better flavoured than those that are found near the sea, as they acquire their excessive fatness by feeding on the wild rice which grows so plentifully in these parts.

Having made some acceptable presents to the good old queen, and received her blessing, I left the town of the Winnebagoes on the 29th of September, and about twelve miles from it arrived at the place where the Fox River enters the Lake on the north side of it. We proceeded up this river, and on the 7th of October reached the great Carrying Place which divides it from the Ouisconsin. This river is the greatest resort for wild fowl of every kind that I met with in the whole course of my travels; frequently the sun would be obscured by them for some minutes together. Deer and bears are very numerous in these parts and a great many beavers and other furs are taken on the streams that empty themselves into this river.

The River is remarkable for having been, about eighty years ago, the residence of the united bands of the Ottagaumies and the Saukies whom the French had nicknamed, according to their wonted custom, Des Sacs and Des Reynards, the Sacks and the Foxes, of whom the following anecdote was related to me by an Indian.

About sixty years ago, the French missionaries and traders having received many insults from these people, a party of French and Indians under the command of Captain Morand marched to revenge their wrongs. The captain set out from the Green Bay in the winter, when they were unsuspicious of a visit of this kind, and pursuing his route over the snow to their villages, which lay about fifty miles up the Fox River, came upon them by surprize. Unprepared as they were, he found them an easy conquest and consequently killed or took prisoners the greatest part of them. On the return of the French to the Green Bay, one of the Indian chiefs in alliance with them, who had a considerable band of the prisoners under his care, stopped to drink at a brook. In the mean time his companions went on which, being observed by one of the women whom they had made captive, she suddenly seized him with both her hands, whilst he stooped to drink, by an exquisitely susceptible part and held him fast till he expired on the spot. As the chief, from the extreme torture he suffered, was unable to call out to his friends or to give any alarm, they passed on without knowing what had happened and the woman, having cut the bands of those of her fellow prisoners who were in the rear, with them made her escape. This heroine was ever after treated by her nation as their deliverer, and made a chiefess in her own right, with liberty to entail the same honour on her descendants, an unusual distinction and permitted only on extraordinary occasions.

Near one half of the way between the Fox and Ouisconsin Rivers is a morass overgrown with a kind of long grass, the rest of it a plain with some oak and pine trees growing thereon. I observed here a great number of rattle-snakes. Mons. Pinnisance, a French trader, told me a remarkable story concerning one of these reptiles, of which he said he was an eyewitness. An Indian belonging to the Menomonie nation, having taken one of them, found means to tame it and when he had done this, treated it as a Deity, calling it his Great Father and carrying it with him in a box wherever he went. This the Indian had done for several summers when Mons. Pinnisance accidentally met with him at this Carrying Place, just as he was setting off for a winter's hunt. The French gentleman was surprized one day to see the Indian place the box which contained his god on the ground and opening the door give him his liberty, telling him whilst he did it to be sure and return by the time he himself should come back, which was to be the month of May following. As this was but October, Monsieur told the Indian, whose simplicity astonished him, that he fancied he might wait long enough when May arrived for the arrival of his Great Father. The Indian was so confident of his creature's obedience that he offered to lay the Frenchman a wager of two gallons of rum that at the time appointed he would come and crawl into his box. This was agreed on and the second week in May following fixed for the determination of the wager.

At that period they both met there again when the Indian set down his box and called for his Great Father. The snake heard him not, and the time being now expired, he acknowledged that he had lost. However, without seeming to be discouraged, he offered to double the bet if his Great Father came not within two days more. This was further agreed on, when behold on the second day, about one o'clock, the snake arrived and, of his own accord, crawled into the box which was placed ready for him. The French gentleman vouched for the truth of this story and from the accounts I have often received of the docility of those creatures, I see no reason to doubt his veracity.

On the 8th of October we got our canoes into the Ouisconsin River, which at this place is more than a hundred yards wide and the next day arrived at the Great Town of the Saukies. This is the largest and best built Indian town I ever saw. It contains about ninety houses, each large enough for several families. These are built of hewn plank neatly joined, and covered with bark so compactly as to keep out the most penetrating rains. Before the doors are placed comfortable sheds in which the inhabitants sit, when the weather will permit, and smoke their pipes. The streets are regular and spacious so that it appears more like a civilized town than the abode of savages. The land near the town is very good. In their plantations, which lie adjacent to their houses and which are neatly laid out, they raise great quantities of Indian corn, beans, melons, &c. so that this place is esteemed the best market for traders to furnish themselves with provisions of any within eight hundred miles of it.

The Saukies can raise about three hundred warriors who are generally employed every summer in making incursions into the territories of the Illinois and Pawnee nations, from whence they return with a great number of slaves. But those people frequently retaliate and, in their turn, destroy many of the Saukies, which I judge to be the reason that they increase no faster.

Whilst I staid here, I took a view of some mountains that lie about fifteen miles to the southward and abound in lead ore. I ascended one of the highest of these and had an extensive view of the country. For many miles nothing was to be seen but lesser mountains which appeared at a distance like haycocks, they being free from trees. Only a few groves of hickery and stunted oaks covered some of the vallies. So plentiful is lead here that I saw large quantities of it lying about the streets in the town belonging to the Saukies, and it seemed to be as good as the produce of other countries.

On the 10th of October we proceeded down the river and the next day reached the first town of the Ottagaumies. This town contained about fifty houses but we found most of them deserted on account of an epidemical disorder that had lately raged among them and carried off more than one half of the inhabitants. The greater part of those who survived had retired into the woods to avoid the contagion.

On the 15th we entered that extensive river, the Mississippi. The Ouisconsin, from the Carrying Place to the part where it falls into the Mississippi, flows with a smooth but a strong current. The water of it is exceedingly clear and through it you may perceive a fine and sandy bottom, tolerably free from rocks. In it are a few islands, the soil of which appeared to be good though somewhat woody. The land near the river also seemed to be, in general, excellent; but that at a distance is very full of mountains where it is said there are many lead mines.

About five miles from the junction of the rivers, I observed the ruins of a large town in a very pleasing situation. On enquiring of the neighbouring Indians why it is thus deserted, I was informed that about thirty years ago, the Great Spirit had appeared on the top of a pyramid of rocks which lay at a little distance from it towards the west and warned them to quit their habitations, for the land on which they were built belonged to him and he had occasion for it. As a proof that he, who gave them these orders, was really the Great Spirit, he further told them that the grass should immediately spring up on those very rocks from whence he now addressed them, which they knew to be bare and barren. The Indians obeyed and soon after discovered that this miraculous alteration had taken place. They shewed me the spot but the growth of the grass appeared to be no ways supernatural. I apprehend this to have been a strategem of the French or Spanish to answer some selfish view; but in what manner they effected their purpose I know not.

This people, soon after their removal, built a town on the bank of the Mississippi near the mouth of the Ouisconsin, at a place called by the French La Praires les Chiens which signifies the Dog Plains. It is a large town and contains about three hundred families. The houses are well built after the Indian manner, and pleasantly situated on a very rich soil from which they raise every necessary of life in great abundance. I saw here many horses of a good size and shape. This town is the great mart where all the adjacent tribes, and even those who inhabit the most remote branches of the Mississippi, annually assemble about the latter end of May, bringing with them their furs to dispose of to the traders. But it is not always that they conclude their sale here; this is determined by a general council of the chiefs who consult whether it would be more conducive to their interest to sell their goods at this place, or carry them on to Louisiana, or Michilimackinac. According to the decision of this council they either proceed further, or return to their different homes.

The Mississippi, at the entrance of the Ouisconsin, near which stands a mountain of considerable height, is about half a mile over. But opposite to the last mentioned town it appears to be more than a mile wide, and full of islands, the soil of which is extraordinary rich and but thinly wooded.

A little farther to the west, on the contrary side, a small river falls into the Mississippi, which the French call Le Jaun Riviere, or the Yellow River. Here the traders who had accompanied me hitherto, took up their residence for the winter. I then bought a canoe, and with two servants, one a French Canadian and the other a Mohawk of Canada, on the 19th proceeded up the Mississippi.

About ten days after I had parted from the traders, I landed as I usually did every evening and, having pitched my tent, I ordered my men when night came on to lay themselves down to sleep. By a light that I kept burning, I then sat down to copy the minutes I had taken in the course of the preceding day. About ten o'clock, having just finished my memorandums, I stepped out of my tent to see what weather it was. As I cast my eyes towards the bank of the river, I thought I saw by the light of the stars, which shone bright, something that had the appearance of a herd of beasts coming down a descent at some distance. Whilst I was wondering what they could be, one of the number suddenly sprung up and discovered to me the form of a man.

In an instant they were all on their legs and I could count about ten or twelve of them running towards me. I immediately reentered the tent and awaking my men ordered them to take their arms and follow me. As my first apprehensions were for my canoe, I ran to the water's side and found a party of Indians (for such I now discovered them to be) on the point of plundering it. Before I reached them, I commanded my men not to fire till I had given the word, being unwilling to begin hostilities unless occasion absolutely required. I accordingly advanced with resolution close to the points of their spears, they had no other weapons, and brandishing my hanger, asked them with a stern voice what they wanted. They were staggered at this and perceiving they were like to meet with a warm reception, turned about and precipitately retreated.

We pursued them to an adjacent wood which they entered and we saw no more of them. However, for fear of their return, we watched alternately during the remainder of the night. The next day, my servants were under great apprehensions and earnestly entreated me to return to the traders we had lately left. But I told them that if they would be esteemed old women (a term of the greatest reproach among the Indians) they must follow me, for I was determined to pursue my intended route, as an Englishman when once engaged in an adventure never retreated. On this they got into the canoe and I walked on the shore to guard them from any further attack.

The party of Indians who had thus intended to plunder me I afterwards found to be some of those straggling bands that have been driven from among the different tribes to which they belonged for various crimes, now associated themselves together and living by plunder, prove very troublesome to travellers who pass this way; nor are even Indians of every tribe spared by them. The traders had before cautioned me to be upon my guard against them and I would repeat the same caution to those whose business might call them into these parts.

On the first of November, I arrived at Lake Pepin, which is rather an extended part of the River Mississippi about two hundred miles from the Ouisconsin. The Mississippi below this Lake flows with a gentle current, but the breadth of it is very uncertain, in some places it being upwards of a mile, in others not more than a quarter. This River has a range of mountains on each side throughout the whole of the way which in particular parts approach near to it, in others lies at a greater distance. The land betwixt the mountains, and on their sides, is generally covered with grass with a few groves of trees interspersed, near which large droves of deer and elk are frequently seen feeding.

In many places pyramids of rocks appeared, resembling old ruinous towers; at others amazing precipices; and what is very remarkable, whilst this scene presented itself on one side, the opposite side of the same mountain was covered with the finest herbage, which gradually ascended to its summit. From thence the most beautiful and extensive prospect that imagination can form opens to your view. Verdant plains, fruitful meadows, numerous islands, and all these abounding with a variety of trees that yield amazing quantities of fruit without care or cultivation, such as the nut-tree, the maple which produces sugar, vines loaded with rich grapes, and plum-trees bending under their blooming burdens, but above all, the fine River flowing gently beneath, and reaching as far as the eye can extend, by turns attract your admiration and excite your wonder.

The Lake abounds with various kinds of fish. Great numbers of fowl frequent also this Lake and rivers adjacent, such as storks, swans, geese, brants, and ducks: and in the groves are found great plenty of turkeys and partridges. On the plains are the largest buffaloes of any in America.

One day, having landed on the shore of the Mississippi, some miles below Lake Pepin, whilst my attendants were preparing my dinner, I walked out to take a view of the adjacent country. I had not proceeded far before I came to a fine, level, open plain on which I perceived at a little distance, a partial elevation that had the appearance of an intrenchment. On a nearer inspection I had greater reason to suppose that it had really been intended for this many centuries ago. Notwithstanding it was now covered with grass, I could plainly discern that it had once been a breast-work of about four feet in height, extending the best part of a mile, and sufficiently capacious to cover five thousand men. Its form was somewhat circular and its flanks reached to the River. Though much defaced by time, every angle was distinguishable and appeared as regular and fashioned with as much military skill as if fashioned by Vauban* himself.

The ditch was not visible, but I thought on examining more curiously that I could perceive there certainly had been one. From its situation also I am convinced that it must have been designed for this purpose. It fronted the country and the rear was covered by the River; nor was there any rising ground for a considerable way that commanded it. A few straggling oaks were alone to be seen near it. In many places small tracks were worn across it by the feet of elks and deer and from the depth of the bed of earth by which it was covered, I was able to draw certain conclusions of its great antiquity.

I examined all the angles and every part with great attention and have often blamed myself since for not encamping on the spot and drawing an exact plan of it. To shew that this description is not the offspring of a heated imagination or the chimerical tale of a mistaken traveller, I find on enquiry since my return that several traders have, at different times, taken notice of similar appearances on which they have formed the same conjectures but without examining them so minutely as I did.

How a work of this kind could exist in a country that has hitherto (according to the general received opinion) been the seat of war to untutored Indians alone, whose whole stock of military knowledge has only, till within two centuries, amounted to drawing the bow, and whose only breast-work even at present is the thicket, I know not. I have given as exact account as possible of this singular appearance and leave to future explorers of these distant regions to discover whether it is a production of nature or art. Perhaps the hint I have here given

* Sebastien le Prestre de Vauban, a celebrated eighteenth-century French military engineer.

might lead to a more perfect investigation of it and give us very different ideas of the ancient state of realms that we at present believe to have been from the earliest period only the habitation of savages.

The Mississippi, as far as the entrance of the River St. Croix, thirty miles above Lake Pepin, is very full of islands. On these, grow numbers of maple or sugar trees, and around them vines loaded with grapes creeping to their very tops. Near the River St. Croix reside three bands of the Naudowessie Indians, called the River Bands.

This nation is composed, at present, of eleven bands. They were originally twelve; but the Assinipoils some years ago revolting, and separating themselves from the others, there remain only at this time eleven. Those I met here are termed River Bands because they dwell near the banks of this River. The other eight are generally distinguished by the title of the Naudowessies of the Plains, and inhabit a country that lies more to the westward.

I fell in with a party amounting to forty warriors and their families. With these I resided a day or two, during which time five or six of their number, who had been out on an excursion, returned in great haste and acquainted their companions that a large party of the Chipeway warriors, "enough," as they expressed themselves, "to swallow them all up," were close at their heels and on the point of attacking their little camp. The chiefs applied to me, and desired I would put myself at their head, and lead them out to oppose their enemies. As I was a stranger, and unwilling to excite the anger of either nation, I knew not how to act and never found myself in a greater dilemma.

Had I refused to assist the Naudowessies I should have drawn on myself their displeasure, or had I met the Chipeways with hostile intentions, I should have made that people my foes, and had I been fortunate enough to have escaped their arrows at this time, on some future occasion should probably have experienced the severity of their revenge. In this extremity, I chose the middle course and desired that the Naudowessies would suffer me to meet them that I might endeavour to avert their fury. To this they reluctantly as-

sented, being persuaded, from the inveteracy which had long prevailed between them, that my remonstrances would be in vain.

Taking my Frenchman with me who could speak their language, I
hastened towards the place where the Chipeways were supposed to be.
The Naudowessies during this kept at a distance behind. As I approached them with the pipe of peace, a small party of their chiefs,
consisting of about eight or ten, came in a friendly manner towards
me with whom, by means of my interpreter, I held a long conversation the result of which was that, their rancour being by my persua-
sions in some measure mollified, they agreed to return back without
accomplishing their savage purposes. During our discourse I could
perceive, as they lay scattered about, that the party was very numerous and many of them armed with muskets.

Having happily succeeded in my undertaking, I returned without
delay to the Naudowessies, and desired they would instantly remove
their camp to some other part of the country, lest their enemies should
repent of the promise they had given and put their intentions in
execution. They accordingly followed my advice and immediately
prepared to strike their tents. Whilst they were doing this they loaded
me with thanks and when I had seen them on board their canoes, I
pursued my route.

To this adventure I was chiefly indebted for the friendly reception
I afterwards met with from the Naudowessies of the Plains, and for
the respect and honours I received during my abode among them.
And when I arrived many months after at the Chipeway village, near
the Ottowaw lakes, I found that my fame had reached that place
before me. The chiefs received me with great cordiality, and the elder
part of them thanked me for the mischief I had prevented. They
informed me, that the war between their nation and the Naudowessies
had continued without interruption for more than forty winters. That
they had long wished to put an end to it, but this was generally
prevented by the young warriors of either nation who could not
restrain their ardour when they met. They said, they should be happy
if some chief of the same pacific disposition as myself, and who

possessed an equal degree of resolution and coolness, would settle in the country between the two nations; for by the interference of such a person an accommodation, which on their parts they sincerely desired, might be brought about. As I did not meet any of the Naudowessies afterwards, I had not an opportunity of forwarding so good a work.

About thirty miles below the Falls of St. Anthony, at which I arrived the tenth day after I left Lake Pepin, is a remarkable cave of an amazing depth. The Indians term it Wakon-teebe, that is, the Dwelling of the Great Spirit. The entrance is about ten feet wide, the height of it five feet. The arch within is near fifteen feet high and about thirty feet broad. The bottom of it consists of fine clear sand. About twenty feet from the entrance begins a lake the water of which is transparent and extends to an unsearchable distance, for the darkness of the cave prevents all attempts to acquire a knowledge of it. I threw a small pebble towards the interior parts of it with my utmost strength. I could hear that it fell into the water and notwithstanding it was so small a size, it caused an astonishing and horrible noise that reverberated through all those gloomy regions.

I found in this cave many Indian hieroglyphicks which appeared very ancient, for time had nearly covered them with moss, so that it was with difficulty I could trace them. They were cut in a rude manner upon the inside of the walls, which were composed of stone so extremely soft that it might be easily penetrated with a knife.

At a little distance from this dreary cavern is the burying-place of several bands of the Naudowessie Indian. Though these people have no fixed residence, living in tents, and abiding but a few months on one spot, they always bring the bones of their dead to this place which they take the opportunity of doing when the chiefs meet to hold their councils and settle all public affairs for the ensuing summer.

Ten miles below the Falls of St. Anthony, the River St. Pierre, called by the natives the Waddapawmenesotor, falls into the Mississippi from the west. Nearly over against this river I was obliged to leave my canoe, on account of the ice, and travel by land to the Falls of

St. Anthony where I arrived on the 17th of November. The Mississippi from the St. Pierre to this place is rather more rapid than I had hitherto found it, and without islands of any consideration.

Before I left my canoe I overtook a young prince of the Winnebagoe Indians, who was going on an embassy to some of the bands of the Naudowessies. Finding that I intended to take a view of the Falls, he agreed to accompany me, his curiosity having been often excited by the accounts he had received from some of his chiefs. He accordingly left his family (for the Indians never travel without their households) at this place under the care of my Mohawk servant and we proceeded together by land, attended only by my Frenchman, to this celebrated place.

We could distinctly hear the noise of the water full fifteen miles before we reached the Falls; and I was greatly pleased and surprized when I approached this astonishing work of nature; but I was not long at liberty to indulge these emotions, my attention being called off by the behaviour of my companion.

The prince had no sooner gained the point that overlooks this wonderful cascade than he began with an audible voice to address the Great Spirit, one of whose places of residence he imagined this to be. He told him that he had come a long way to pay his adorations to him and now would make him the best offerings in his power. He accordingly first threw his pipe into the stream, then the roll that contained his tobacco; after these, the bracelets he wore on his arms and wrists; next an ornament that encircled his neck, composed of beads and wires; and at last the ear-rings from his ears. In short, he presented to his god every part of his dress that was valuable; during this he frequently smote his breast with great violence, threw his arms about, and appeared to be much agitated.

All this while he continued his adorations and at length concluded them with fervent petitions that the Great Spirit would constantly afford us his protection on our travels, giving us a bright sun, a blue sky, and clear untroubled waters; nor would he leave the place till we had smoked together with my pipe in honour of the Great Spirit.

I was greatly surprized at beholding an instance of such elevated devotion in so young an Indian and instead of ridiculing the ceremonies attending it, as I observed my Catholic servant tacitly did, I looked on the prince with a greater degree of respect for these sincere proofs he gave of his piety, and I doubt not but that his offerings and prayers were as acceptable to the universal Parent of mankind as if they had been made with greater pomp or in a consecrated place.

Indeed, the whole conduct of this young prince at once amazed and charmed me. During the few days we were together, his attention seemed totally to be employed in yielding me every assistance in his power and even in so short a time, he gave me innumerable proofs of the most generous and disinterested friendship so that on our return, I parted from him with great reluctance. Whilst I beheld the artless yet engaging manners of this unpolished savage, I could not help drawing a comparison between him and some of the more refined inhabitants of civilized countries.

The Falls of St. Anthony received their name from Father Louis Hennepin, a French missionary who travelled into these parts about the year 1680 and was the first European ever seen by the natives. The country around the Falls is extremely beautiful. It is not an uninterrupted plain where the eye finds no relief, but composed of many gentle ascents, which in the summer are covered with the finest verdure, and interspersed with little groves, that give a pleasing variety to the prospect. On the whole, when the Falls are included, which may be seen at the distance of four miles, a more pleasing and picturesque view cannot, I believe, be found throughout the universe. I could have wished that I had happened to enjoy this glorious sight at a more seasonable time of the year, whilst the trees and hollocks were clad in nature's gayest livery, as this must have greatly added to the pleasure I received.

At a little distance below the Falls stands a small island of about an acre and a half on which grow a great number of oak trees, every branch of which, able to support the weight, was full of eagles nests. The reason that this kind of bird resorts in such numbers to this spot is that they are here secure from the attacks either of man or beast, their

surveyed by Capt. Carver, Nov. 17, 1766.

The Falls of St. Anthony in the River MISSISSIPPI,
near 2400 Miles from its entrance into the Gulf of Mexico.

Mr. J. Fenton Sculpt.

Height of the Fall
30 Feet Perpend.

Breadth, near
600 Feet.

85

retreat being guarded by the Rapids, which the Indians never attempt to pass. Another reason is that they find a constant supply of food for themselves and their young from the animals and fish which are dashed to pieces by the Falls and driven on the adjacent shore.

Having satisfied my curiosity, as far as the eye of man can be satisfied, I proceeded on till I reached the River St. Francis, near sixty miles above the Falls. As the season was so advanced, and the weather extremely cold, I was not able to make so many observations of these parts as I otherwise should have done. The country in some places is hilly, but without large mountains, and the land is tolerably good. I observed here many deer and carribboos, some elk, with abundance of beavers, otters, and other furs. A little above this, to the north-east, are a number of small lakes called the Thousand Lakes, the parts about which, though but little frequented, are the best within many miles for hunting, as the hunter never fails of returning loaded beyond his expectations.

The River St. Pierre, at its junction with the Mississippi, is about a hundred yards broad. It has a great depth of water and in some places runs very briskly. I proceeded up this river about two hundred miles to the country of the Naudowessies of the Plains. On the 7th of December, I arrived at the utmost extent of my travels towards the west where I met with a large party of Naudowessies among whom I resided five months. These constituted a part of the eight bands of the Naudowessies of the Plains. The Naudowessie nation, when united consists of more than two thousand warriors. The Assinipoils, who revolted from them, amount to about three hundred and leagued with the Killistinoes, live in a continual state of enmity with the other bands.

As I proceeded up the River St. Pierre, and had nearly reached the place where these people were encamped, I observed two or three canoes coming down the stream. No sooner had the Indians that were on board them discovered us than they rowed toward the land and, leaping ashore with precipitation, left their canoes to float as the current drove them. In a few minutes I perceived some others who, as soon as they came in sight, followed with equal speed the example of their countrymen.

I now thought it necessary to proceed with caution; and therefore kept on the side of the river opposite to that on which the Indians had landed. However, I still continued my course, satisfied that the pipe of Peace which was fixed at the head of my canoe and the English colours that were flying at the stern would prove my security. After rowing about half a mile farther, in turning a point, I discovered a great number of tents and more than a thousand Indians at a little distance from the shore. Being now nearly opposite to them, I ordered my men to pull directly over, as I was willing to convince the Indians by such a step that I placed some confidence in them.

As soon as I had reached the land, two of the chiefs presented their hands to me and led me, amidst the astonished multitude who had most of them never seen a white man before, to a tent. Into this we entered, and according to the custom that universally prevails among every Indian nation, began to smoke the pipe of Peace. We had not sat long before the crowd became so great, both around and upon the tent, that we were in danger of being crushed by its fall. On this we returned to the plain where, having gratified the curiosity of the common people, their wonder abated and ever after they treated me with great respect.

From the chiefs I met with the most friendly and hospitable reception which induced me, as the season was so far advanced, to take up my residence among them during the winter. To render my stay as comfortable as possible, I first endeavoured to learn their language. This I soon did, so as to make myself perfectly intelligible, having before acquired some slight knowledge of the language of those Indians that live on the back of the settlements; and in consequence met with every accommodation their manner of living would afford. Nor did I want for such amusements as tended to make so long a period pass cheerfully away. I frequently hunted with them; and at other times beheld with pleasure their recreations and pastimes, which I shall describe hereafter.

Sometimes I sat with the chiefs and, whilst we smoked the friendly pipe, entertained them in return for the accounts they gave me of their wars and excursions with a narrative of my own adventures and a description of all the battles fought between the English and the French in America, in many of which I had a personal share. They always paid great attention to my details, and asked many pertinent questions relative to the European methods of making war.

I held these conversations with them in a great measure to procure from them some information relative to the chief point I had constantly in view, that of gaining a knowledge of the situation and produce, both of their own country and those that lay to the westward of them. Nor was I disappointed in my designs, for I procured from them much useful intelligence. They likewise drew for me plans of all the countries with which they were acquainted but as I entertained no great opinion of their geographical knowledge, I placed not much dependence on them. They draw with a piece of burnt coal, taken from the hearth, upon the inside bark of the birch tree which is as smooth as paper and answers the same purpose, notwithstanding it is of a yellow cast. Their sketches are made in a rude manner, but they seem to give as just an idea of a country, although the plan is not so exact as more experienced draughtsmen could do.

I left the habitations of these hospitable Indians the latter end of April 1767; but did not part from them for several days, as I was accompanied on my journey by near three hundred of them, among whom were many chiefs, to the mouth of the River St. Pierre. At this season, these bands annually go to the Great Cave, before mentioned, to hold a grand council with all the other bands, wherein they settle their operations for the ensuing year. At the same time they carry with them their dead for interment bound up in buffaloes skins.

Never did I travel with so cheerful and happy a company. But their mirth met with a sudden and temporary allay from a violent storm that overtook us one day on our passage. We had just landed, and were preparing to set up our tents for the night, when a heavy cloud overspread the heavens and the most dreadful thunder, lightening, and rain issued from it that ever I beheld.

The Indians were greatly terrified, and ran to such shelter as they could find; for only a few tents were as yet erected. Apprehensive of the danger that might ensue from standing near any thing which could serve for a conductor, as the cloud appeared to contain such an uncommon quantity of electrical fluid, I took my stand as far as possible from any covering, chusing rather to be exposed to the peltings of the storm than to receive a fatal stroke. At this the Indians were greatly surprized, and drew conclusions from it not unfavourable to the opinion they already entertained of my resolution. Yet I acknowledge that I was never more affected in my life, for nothing scarcely could exceed the terrific scene. The peals of thunder were so loud that they shook the earth and the lightening flashed along the ground in streams of sulphur so that the Indian chiefs themselves, although their courage in war is usually invincible, could not help trembling at the horrid combustion. As soon as the storm was over, they flocked around me and informed me that it was proof of the anger of the evil spirits whom they were apprehensive that they had highly offended.

When we arrived at the Great Cave, and the Indians had deposited the remains of their deceased friends in the burial-place that stands adjacent to it, they held their great council into which I was admitted and, at the same time, had the honour to be installed or adopted a chief of their bands. On this occasion, I made the following speech which I insert to give my Readers a specimen of the language and manner in which it is necessary to address the Indians so as to engage their attention and to render the speaker's expressions consonant to their ideas.

My brothers, chiefs of the numerous and powerful Naudowessies! I rejoice that through my long abode with you, I can now speak to you (though after an imperfect manner) in your own tongue, like one of your own children. I rejoice also that I have had an opportunity so frequently to inform you of the glory and power of the Great King that reigns over the English and other nations; who is descended from a very ancient race of sovereigns, as old as the earth and waters; whose feet stand on two great islands, larger than any you have ever seen, amidst the greatest waters in the world; whose head reaches to the sun and whose arms encircle the whole earth. The number of whose warriors are equal to the trees in the vallies, the stalks of rice in yonder marshes, or the blades of grass on your great plains. Who has hundreds of canoes of his own, of such amazing bigness that all the waters in your country would not suffice for one of them to swim in; each of which have guns not small like mine which you see before you, but of such magnitude that a hundred of your stoutest young men would with difficulty be able to carry one. And these are equally surprizing in their operation against the Great King's enemies when engaged in battle. The terror they carry with them your language wants words to express. You may remember the other day when we were camping at Waddapawmenesotor, the black clouds, the wind, the fire, the stupendous noise, the horrible cracks, and the trembling of the earth which then alarmed you, and gave you reason to think your gods were angry with you. Not unlike these are the war-like implements of the English when they are fighting the battles of their Great King. Several of the chiefs of your bands have often told me in times past, when I dwelt with you in your tents, that they much wished to be counted among the children and allies of the Great King, my master. You may remember how often you have desired me, when I return again to my own country, to acquaint the great King of your good disposition towards him and his subjects, and that you wished for traders from the English to come among you. But now about to take my leave of you and to return to my own country, a long way towards the rising sun, I again ask you to tell me whether you continue of the same mind as when I spoke to you in council last winter; and as there are now several of your chiefs here who came from the great plains toward the setting of the sun whom I have never spoke with in council before, I ask you to let me know if you are willing to acknowledge yourselves the children of my great master, the King of the English and other nations, as I shall take the first opportunity to acquaint him of your desires and good intentions. I charge you not to give heed to bad reports, for there are wicked birds flying about among the neighbouring nations who may whisper evil things in your ears against the English, contrary to what I have told you. You must not believe them for I have told you the truth. And as for the chiefs that are about to go to Michilimackinac, I shall take care to make for them and their suite a straight road, smooth waters, and a clear sky, that they may go there and smoke the pipe of Peace, and rest secure on a beaver blanket under the shade of the great tree of peace. Farewell.

To this speech, I received the following answer from the mouth of the principal chief.

Good brother! I am now about to speak to you with the mouths of these, my brothers, chiefs of the eight bands of the powerful nation of the Naudowessies. We believe and are well satisfied in the truth of every thing you have told us about your great nation and the Great King, our greatest father, for whom we spread this beaver blanket that his fatherly protection may ever rest easy and safe amongst us, his children. Your colours and your arms agree with the accounts you have given us about your great nation. We desire that when you return, you will acquaint the Great King how much the Naudowessies wish to be counted among his good children. You may believe us when we tell you that we will not open our ears to any who may dare to speak evil of our Great Father, the King of the English and other nations. We thank you for what you have done for us in making peace between the Naudowessies and the Chipeways and hope when you return to us again that you will complete this good work and, quite dispelling the clouds that intervene, open the blue sky of peace and cause the bloody hatchet to be deep buried under the roots of the great tree of peace. We wish you to remember to represent to our Great Father how much we desire that traders may be sent to abide among us with such things as we need, that the hearts of our young men, our wives and children may be made glad. And may peace subsist between us, so long as the sun, the moon, the earth, and the waters shall endure. Farewell.

I thought it necessary to caution the Indians against giving heed to any bad reports that may reach them from the neighbouring nations to the disadvantage of the English as I had heard, at different places through which I passed, that emissaries were still employed by the French to detach those who were friendly to the English from their interest. And I saw myself several belts of wampum that had been delivered for this purpose to some of the tribes I was among. On the delivery of each of these, a Talk was held wherein the Indians were told that the English, who were but a petty people, had stolen that country from their Great Father, the king of France, whilst he was asleep but that he would soon awake and take them again under his protection.

Whilst I tarried at the mouth of the River St. Pierre with these friendly Indians, I endeavoured to gain intelligence whether any goods had been sent towards the Falls of St. Anthony for my use, agreeable to the promise I had received from the governor when I left Michilimackinac. But finding from some Indians who passed by in their return from those parts that this agreement had not been fulfilled, I was obliged to give up all thoughts of proceeding farther to the north-west by this route. I therefore returned to La Prairie le Chien where I procured as many goods from the traders I left there the preceding year as they could spare.

As these however were not sufficient to enable me to renew my first design, I determined to endeavour to make my way across the country of the Chipeways to Lake Superior in hopes of meeting at the Grand Portage on the north side of it the traders that annually go from Michilimackinac to the north-west, of whom I doubted not but that I should be able to procure goods enough to answer my purpose, and also to penetrate through those more northern parts to the Straits of Annian.

I reached the eastern side of Lake Pepin where I went ashore and encamped as usual. The next morning, when I had proceeded some miles farther, I perceived at a distance before me a smoke, which denoted that some Indians were near and in a short time discovered ten or twelve tents not far from the bank of the river. As I was apprehensive that this was a party of the Rovers I had before met with, I knew not what course to pursue. My attendants persuaded me to endeavour to pass by them on the opposite side of the river, but as I had hitherto found that the best way to ensure a friendly reception from the Indians is to meet them boldly, and without shewing any tokens of fear, I would by no means consent to their proposal. Instead of this I crossed directly over, and landed in the middle of them, for by this time the greatest part of them were standing on the shore.

The first I accosted were Chipeways inhabiting near the Ottowaw lakes; who received me with great cordiality, and shook me by the hand in token of friendship. At some distance behind these stood a chief remarkably tall and well made, but of so stern an aspect that the most undaunted person could not behold him without feeling some degree of terror. He seemed to have passed the meridian of life and by the mode in which he was painted and tatowed, I discovered that he was of high rank. However, I approached him in a courteous manner, and expected to have met with the same reception I had done from the others. But to my great surprize he with-held his hand and, looking fiercely at me, said in the Chipeway tongue, "Cawin nish-ishin saganosh," that is, "The English are no good." As he had his tomahawk in his hand, I expected that this laconick sentence would have been followed by a blow, to prevent which I drew a pistol from my belt and, holding it in a careless position, passed close by him to let him see I was not afraid of him.

I learned soon after from the other Indians, that this was a chief, called by the French the Grand Sautor or the Great Chipeway Chief. They likewise told me that he had been always a steady friend to that people, and when they delivered up Michilimackinac to the English on their evacuation of Canada, the Grand Sautor had sworn that he would ever remain the avowed enemy of its new possessors, as the territories on which the fort is built belonged to him.

Finding him thus disposed, I took care to be constantly upon my guard whilst I staid; but that he might not suppose I was driven away by his frowns, I took up my abode there for the night. I pitched my tent at some distance from the Indians and had no sooner laid myself down to rest than I was awakened by my French servant. Having been alarmed by the sound of Indian music, he had run to the outside of the tent where he beheld a party of the young savages dancing towards us in an extraordinary manner, each carrying in his hand a torch fixed on the top of a long pole. But I shall defer any further account of this uncommon entertainment, which at once surprized and alarmed me, till I treat of the Indian dances.

The next morning I continued my voyage and before night reached La Prairie le Chien. Since I came to England, I have been informed that the Grand Sautor was at length stabbed in his tent as he encamped near Michilimackinac by a trader. I should have remarked that whatever Indians happen to meet at La Prairie le Chien, the great mart to which all who inhabit the adjacent countries resort, though the nations to which they belong are at war with each other, yet they are obliged to restrain their enmity, and forbear all hostile acts during their stay there. This regulation has been long established among them for their mutual convenience, as without it no trade could be carried on. The same rule is observed also at the Red Mountain (afterwards described) from whence they get the stone of which they make their pipes: these being indispensable to the accommodation of every neighbouring tribe and is of public utility.

The River St. Pierre, which runs through the territories of the Naudowessies, flows through a most delightful country, abounding with all the necessaries of life that grow spontaneously and, with a little cultivation, it might be made to produce even the luxuries of life. Wild rice grows here in great abundance and every part is filled with trees bending under their loads of fruits, such as plums, grapes, and apples; the meadows are covered with hops and many sorts of vegetables; whilst the ground is stored with useful roots, with angelica, spikenard, and ground-nuts as large as hens eggs. At a little distance from the sides of the river are eminences from which you have views that cannot be exceeded, even by the most beautiful of those I have already described. Amidst these are delightful groves and such amazing quantities of maples that they would produce sugar sufficient for any number of inhabitants.

Near the branch which is termed Marble River is a mountain from whence the Indians get a sort of red stone, out of which they hew the bowls of their pipes. In some of these parts is found a black hard clay, or rather stone, of which the Naudowessies make their family utensils. This country likewise abounds with a milk-white clay of which China ware might be made equal in goodness to the Asiatic, and also with a blue clay that serves the Indians for paint. With this last they contrive, by mixing it with the red stone powdered, to paint themselves of different colours. Those that can get the blue clay here mentioned paint themselves very much with it, particularly when they are about to begin their sports and pastimes. It is also esteemed by them a mark of peace, as it has a resemblance of a blue sky which with them is a symbol of it, and made use of in their speeches as a figurative expression to denote peace. When they wish to shew that their inclinations are pacific towards other tribes, they greatly ornament both themselves and their belts with it.

Having concluded my business at La Prairie le Chien, I proceeded once more up the Mississippi as far as the place where the Chipeway River enters it a little below Lake Pepin. Here, having engaged an Indian pilot, I directed him to steer towards the Ottowaw Lakes which lie near the head of this river.

Near it is a town of the Chipeways from whence the river takes its name. It is situated on each side of the river and lies adjacent to the banks of a small lake. This town contains about forty houses and can send out upwards of one hundred warriors, many of whom were fine stout young men. The houses of it are built after the Indian manner and have neat plantations behind them; but the inhabitants, in general, seemed to be the nastiest people I had ever been among. I observed that the women and children indulged themselves in a custom which though common in some degree throughout every Indian nation, appears to be, according to our ideas, of the most nauseous and indelicate nature, that of searching each other's head and eating the prey caught therein.

In July I left this town, and having crossed a number of small lakes and carrying places that intervened, came to a head branch of the River St. Croix. This branch I descended to a fork, and then ascended another to its source. On both these rivers I discovered several mines of virgin copper which was as pure as that found in any other country.

Here I came to a small brook, which my guide thought might be joined at some distance by streams that would at length render it navigable. The water at first was so scanty that my canoe would by no means swim in it. But having stopped up several old beaver dams which had been broken down by hunters, I was enabled to proceed some miles till by the conjunction of a few brooks, these aids became no longer necessary. In a short time, the water increased to a most rapid river, which we descended till it entered Lake Superior.

The country from the Ottowaw Lakes to Lake Superior is in general very uneven and thickly covered with woods; the soil in some places tolerably good, in others but indifferent. In the heads of the St. Croix and the Chipeway Rivers are exceedingly fine sturgeon. All the wilderness between the Mississippi and Lake Superior is called by the Indians the Moschettoe country and I thought it most justly named; for it being then their season, I never saw or felt so many of those insects in my life.

The latter end of July I arrived, after having coasted through West Bay, at the Grand Portage which lies on the northwest borders of Lake Superior. At the Grand Portage is a small bay before the entrance of which lies an island that intercepts the dreary and uninterrupted view over the Lake which otherwise would have presented itself and makes the bay serene and pleasant. Here I met a large party of Killistinoe and Assinipoil Indians with their respective kings and their families. They were come to this place in order to meet the traders from Michilimackinac who make this their road to the northwest.

These Indians informed me that some of the northern branches of the Messorie and the southern branches of the St. Pierre Rivers have a communication with each other, except for a mile over which they carry their canoes. And by what I could learn from them, this is the road they take when their war parties make their excursions upon the Pawnees and Pawnawnees, nations inhabiting some branches of the Messorie River. In the country belonging to these people it is said that Mandrakes are frequently found, a species of root resembling human beings of both sexes, and that these are more perfect than such as are discovered about the Nile and Nether-Ethiopia.

A little to the north-west of the heads of the Messorie and the St. Pierre, the Indians further told me that there was a nation rather smaller and whiter than the neighbouring tribes who cultivate the ground and (as far as I could gather from their expressions) in some measure, the arts. To this account they added that some of the nations who inhabit those parts that lie to the west of the Shining Mountains have gold so plenty among them that they make their most common utensils of it. These mountains (which I shall describe more particularly hereafter) divide the waters that fall into the South Sea from those that run into the Atlantic.

The people dwelling near them are supposed to be some of the different tribes that were tributary to the Mexican kings and who fled from their native country to seek asylum in these parts, about the time of the conquest of Mexico by the Spaniards more than two centuries ago.

As some confirmation of this supposition it is remarked, that they have chosen the most interior parts for their retreat, being still pre-possessed with a notion that the sea-coasts have been infested ever since with monsters vomiting fire and hurling about thunder and lightening, from whose bowels issued men who, with unseen instruments or by the power of magick, killed the harmless Indians at an astonishing distance. From such as these, their fore-fathers (according to a tradition among them that still remains unimpaired) fled to the retired abodes they now inhabit. For as they found that the floating monsters which had thus terrified them could not approach the land, and that those who had descended from their sides did not care to make excursions to any considerable distance from them, they formed a resolution to betake themselves to some country that lay far from the seacoasts, where only they could be secure from such diabolical enemies. They accordingly set out with their families and, after a long peregrination, settled themselves near these mountains where they concluded they had found a place of perfect security.

The Winnebagoes, dwelling on the Fox River are likewise supposed to be some strolling band from the Mexican countries. But they are able to give only an imperfect account of their original residence. They say they formerly came a great way from the westward, and were driven by wars to take refuge among the Naudowessies. But as they are entirely ignorant of the arts or of the value of gold, it is rather to be supposed that they were driven from their ancient settlements by the above-mentioned emigrants as they passed on towards their present habitation.

These suppositions, however, may want confirmation, for the smaller tribes of Indians are subject to such various alterations in their places of abode from the wars they are continually engaged in, that it is almost impossible to ascertain after half a century the original situation of any of them.

That range of mountains, of which the Shining Mountains are a part, begin at Mexico, and continue northward to the east of California. They are called the Shining Mountains from an infinite number of chrystal stones, of an amazing size with which they are covered and which, when the sun shines full upon them, sparkle so as to be seen at a very great distance.

Probably in future ages, this extraordinary range of mountains may be found to contain more riches in their bowels than those of Indostan and Malabar or that are produced on the Golden Coast of Guinea; nor will I except even the Peruvian Mines. To the west of these mountains, when explored by future Columbuses or Raleighs, may be found other lakes, rivers, and countries, full fraught with all the necessary luxuries of life and where future generations may find an asylum, whether driven from their country by the ravages of lawless tyrants, or by religious persecutions, or reluctantly leaving it to remedy the inconveniences arising from a superabundant increase of inhabitants; whether, I say, impelled by these or allured by hopes of commercial advantages, there is little doubt but their expectations will be fully gratified in these rich and unexhausted climes.

But to return to the Assinipoils and Killistinoes whom I left at the Grand Portage, and from whom I received an account of the lakes that lie to the northwest of this place. The traders we expected being later this season than usual, and our numbers very considerable, for there were more than three hundred of us, the stock of provisions we had brought with us was nearly exhausted, and we waited with impatience for their arrival.

One day, whilst we were expressing our wishes for this desirable event and looking from an eminence in hopes of seeing them come over the lake, the chief priest belonging to the band of the Killistinoes told us that he would endeavour to obtain a conference with the Great Spirit and know from him when the traders would arrive. I paid little attention to this declaration, supposing that it would be productive of some juggling trick, just sufficiently covered to deceive the ignorant Indians. But the king of that tribe telling me that this was chiefly undertaken by the priest to alleviate my anxiety and at the same time to convince me how much interest he had with the Great Spirit, I thought it necessary to refrain my animadversions on his design.

The following evening was fixed upon for this spiritual conference. When every thing had been properly prepared, the king came to me and led me to a capacious tent, the covering of which was drawn up so as to render what was transacting within visible to those who stood without. We found the tent surrounded by a great number of Indians, but we readily gained admission and seated ourselves on skins laid on the ground for that purpose.

In the centre I observed that there was a place for an oblong shape which was composed of stakes stuck in the ground, with intervals between so as to form a kind of chest or coffin, large enough to contain the body of a man. These were of a middle size and placed at such a distance from each other that whatever lay within them was readily to be discerned. The tent was perfectly illuminated by a great number of torches made of splinters cut from the pine or birch tree which the Indians held in their hands.

In a few minutes the priest entered. An amazing large elk's skin being spread on the ground, just at my feet, he laid himself down upon it after having stript himself of every garment except that which he wore close about his middle. Being now prostrate on his back, he first laid hold of one side of the skin and folded it over him, and then the other, leaving only his head uncovered. This was no sooner done, than two of the young men who stood by took about forty yards of strong cord, made also of an elk's hide, and rolled it tight round his body so that he was completely swathed within the skin. Being thus bound up like an Egyptian Mummy, one took him by the heels and the other by the head and lifted him over the pales into the inclosure. I could also now discern him as plain as I had hitherto done and I took care not to turn my eyes a moment from the object before me, that I might the more readily detect the artifice, for such I doubted not but that it would turn out to be.

The priest had not lain in this situation more than a few seconds, when he began to mutter. This he continued to do for some time, and then by degrees grew louder and louder, till at length he spoke articulately; however what he uttered was in such a mixed jargon of the Chipeway, Ottowaw, and Killistinoe languages that I could understand but very little of it. Having continued in this tone for a considerable while, he at last exerted his voice to its utmost pitch, till he had worked himself into such agitation that he foamed at his mouth.

After having remained near three quarters of an hour in the place, and continued his vociferation with unabated vigor, he seemed to be quite exhausted and remained speechless. But in an instant he sprung upon his feet, notwithstanding at the time he was put in, it appeared impossible for him to move either his legs or arms, and shaking off his covering as quick as if the bands with which it had been bound were burned asunder, he began to address those who stood around in a firm and audible voice. "My Brothers," said he, "the Great Spirit has deigned to hold a Talk with his servant at my earnest request. He has not, indeed, told me when the persons we expect will be here, but to-morrow, soon after the sun has reached his highest point in the heavens, a canoe will arrive, and the people in that will inform us when the traders will come." Having said this, he stepped out of the inclosure and after he had put on his robes, dismissed the assembly. I own I was greatly astonished at what I had seen. But as I observed that every eye in the company was fixed on me with a view to discover my sentiments, I carefully concealed every emotion.

The next day the sun shone bright, and long before noon all the Indians were gathered together on the eminence that overlooked the lake. The old king came to me and asked me whether I had so much confidence in what the priest had foretold as to join his people on the hill and wait for the completion of it. I told him I was at a loss what opinion to form of the prediction, but that I would readily attend him. On this we walked together to the place where the others were assembled. Every eye was again fixed by turns on me and on the lake when, just as the sun had reached his zenith, agreeable to what the priest had foretold, a canoe came round a point of land about a league distant. The Indians no sooner beheld it than they sent up an universal shout, and by their looks seemed to triumph in the interest their priest thus evidently had with the Great Spirit.

In less than an hour the canoe reached the shore, when I attended the king and chiefs to receive those who were on board. As soon as the men were landed, we walked all together to the king's tent when, according to their invariable custom we began to smoke; and this we did, notwithstanding our impatience to know the tidings they brought, without asking any questions for the Indians are the most deliberate people in the world. However, after some trivial conversation, the king inquired of them whether they had seen any thing of the traders. The men replied that they had parted from them a few days before and that they proposed being here the second day from the present. They accordingly arrived at that time greatly to our satisfaction, but more particularly so to that of the Indians who found by this event the importance both of their priest and of their nation greatly augmented in the sight of a stranger.

This story I acknowledge appears to carry with it marks of great credulity in the relator. But no one is less tinctured with that weakness than myself. The circumstances of it I own are of a very extraordinary nature; however, as I can vouch for their being free from either exaggeration or misrepresentation, being myself a cool and dispassionate observer of them all, I thought it necessary to give them to the public. And this I do without wishing to mislead the judgment of my Readers or to make superstititous impressions on their minds, but leaving them to draw from it what conclusions they please.

The anxiety I had felt on account of the traders delay, was not much alleviated by their arrival. I again found my expectations disappointed, for I was not able to procure the goods I wanted from any of them. I was therefore obliged to give over my designs and return to the place from whence I first began my extensive circuit. I accordingly took leave of the old king of the Killistinoes, with the chiefs of both bands, and departed. This prince was upwards of sixty years of age, tall and slightly made, but he carried himself very erect. He was of a courteous, affable disposition, and treated me, as did all the chiefs, with great civility.

I observed that this people still continued a custom, that appeared to have been universal before any of them became acquainted with the manners of the Europeans, that of complimenting strangers with the company of their wives. This is not only practised by the lower ranks, but by the chiefs themselves, who esteem it the greatest proof of courtesy they can give a stranger.

After having coasted round the north and east borders of Lake Superior, I arrived at Cadot's Fort which adjoins to the Falls of St. Marie and is situated near the south-west corner of it. Lake Superior, formerly termed the Upper Lake from its northern situation, is so called on account of its being superior in magnitude to any of the lakes on that vast continent. It might justly be termed the Caspian of America. After I first entered it, I observed that the greatest part of that extensive tract was bounded by rocks and uneven ground. The water in general appeared to lie on a bed of rocks. When it was calm and the sun shone bright, I could sit in my canoe, where the depth was upwards of six fathoms, and plainly see huge piles of stone at the bottom of different shapes, some of which appeared as if they were hewn. The water at this time was as pure and transparent as air and my canoe seemed as if it hung suspended in that element. It was impossible to look attentively through this limpid medium at the rocks below without finding, before many minutes had elapsed, your head swim and your eyes no longer able to behold the dazzling scene.

I discovered also by accident another extraordinary property in the waters of this Lake. Though it was in the month of July that I passed over it and the surface of the water, from the heat of the superambient air, impregnated with no small degree of warmth, yet on letting down a cup to the depth of about a fathom, the water drawn from thence was so excessively cold that it had the same effect when received into the mouth as ice.

There are many islands in this Lake. One of the Chipeway chiefs told me that some of their people being once driven on the island of Mauropas, which lies towards the north-east part of the Lake, found on it large quantities of a heavy shining yellow sand that from their description must have been gold dust. Being struck with the beautiful appearance of it, in the morning when they re-entered their canoe, they attempted to bring some away. But a spirit of amazing size, according to their account sixty feet in height, strode into the water after them and commanded them to deliver back what they had taken away. Terrified at his gigantic stature, and seeing that he had nearly overtaken them, they were glad to restore their shining treasure, on which they were suffered to depart without further molestation. Since this incident, no Indian that has ever heard of it will venture near the same haunted coast. Besides this, they recounted to me many other stories of these islands, equally fabulous.

Lake Huron, into which you now enter from the Straits of St. Marie, is the next in magnitude to Lake Superior. The promontory that separates this lake from Lake Michigan is composed of a vast plain, upwards of one hundred miles long, but varying in its breadth, being from ten to fifteen miles broad. This track is divided into almost an equal portion between the Ottowaw and Chipeway Indians. At the north-east corner this lake has a communication with Lake Michigan, by the Straits of Michilimackinac.

From the Falls of St. Marie I leisurely proceeded back to Michilimackinac, and arrived there the beginning of November 1767, having been fourteen months on this extensive tour, travelled near four thousand miles, and visited twelve nations of Indians lying to the west and north of this place. The winter setting in soon after my arrival, I was obliged to tarry there till the June following, the navigation over Lake Huron for large vessels not being open, on account of the ice, till that time. Meeting here with sociable company, I passed these months very agreeably and without finding the hours tedious.

One of my chief amusements was that of fishing for trouts. Though the Straits were covered with ice, we found means to make holes through it and letting down strong lines of fifteen yards in length, to which were fixed three or four hooks baited with small fish, we frequently caught two at a time of forty pounds weight each; but the common size is from ten to twenty pounds. The method of preserving them during the three months the winter generally lasts is by hanging them up in the air and in one night they will be frozen so hard that they will keep as well as if they were cured with salt.

In June 1768 I left Michilimackinac and returned in the Gladwyn Schooner, a vessel of about eighty tons burthen, over Lake Huron to Lake St. Claire where we left the ship and proceeded in boats to Detroit. The banks of the River Detroit are covered with settlements that extend more than twenty miles, the country being exceedingly fruitful and proper for the cultivation of wheat, Indian corn, oats, and peas. It has also many spots of fine pasturage. But as the inhabitants, who are chiefly French that submitted to the English government after the conquest of these parts by General Amherst, are more attentive to the Indian trade than to farming, it is but badly cultivated.

The town of Detroit contains upwards of one hundred houses. The streets are somewhat regular and have a range of very convenient and handsome barracks, with a spacious parade at the south end. On the west side lies the King's garden belonging to the governor, which is very well laid out and kept in good order. The fortifications of the town consist of a strong stockade made of round piles fixed firmly in the ground and lined with palisades. These are defended by some small bastions on which are mounted a few indifferent cannon of an inconsiderable size, just sufficient for its defence against the Indians or an enemy not provided with artillery.

The garrison, in time of peace, consists of two hundred men commanded by a field officer, who acts as chief magistrate under the governor of Canada. Mr. Turnbull, the captain of the 60th regiment or Royal Americans, was commandant when I happened to be there. This gentleman was deservedly esteemed and respected, both by the inhabitants and traders, for the propriety of his conduct and I am happy to have an opportunity of thus publickly making my acknowledgments to him for the civilities I received from him during my stay.

In the year 1762, in the month of July, it rained on this town and the parts adjacent a sulphureous water of the colour and consistence of ink, some of which, being collected into bottles and wrote with, appeared perfectly intelligible on paper and answered every purpose of that useful liquid. Soon after, the Indian wars broke out in these parts. I mean not to say that this incident was ominous of them, notwithstanding it is well known that innumerable well attested instances of extraordinary phaenomena happening before extraordinary events have been recorded in almost every age by historians of veracity. I only relate the circumstances as a fact of which I was informed by many persons of undoubted probity and leave my Readers, as I have hitherto done, to draw their own conclusions from it.

Lake Erie receives the waters by which it is supplied from the three great lakes, through the Straits of Detroit that lie at its northwest corner. There are several islands near the west end of it so infested with rattle-snakes that it is very dangerous to land on them. It is impossible that any place can produce a greater number of all kinds of these reptiles than this does, particularly the water-snake. The Lake is covered near the banks of the islands with the large pond-lily, the leaves of which lie on the surface of the water so thick as to cover it entirely for many acres together; and on each of these lay, when I passed over it, wreaths of water-snakes basking in the sun, which amounted to myriads.

The most remarkable of the different species that infest this Lake is the hissing-snake which is of the small speckled kind, and about eighteen inches long. When any thing approaches, it flattens itself in a moment and its spots, which are of various dyes, become visibly brighter through rage. At the same time it blows from its mouth with great force a subtile wind that is reported to be of a nauseous smell and, if drawn in with the breath of the unwary traveller, will infallibly bring on a decline that in a few months must prove mortal, there being no remedy yet discovered which can counteract its baneful influence.

The navigation of this Lake is esteemed more dangerous than any of the others on account of many high lands that lie on the borders of it, and project into the water in a perpendicular direction for many miles together so that whenever sudden storms arise, canoes and boats are frequently lost as there is no place for them to find a shelter.

This Lake discharges its waters at the north-east end into the River Niagara from whence it falls into Lake Ontario. At the entrance of this river, on its eastern shore, lies Fort Niagara and about eighteen miles further up, those remarkable Falls which are esteemed one of the most extraordinary productions of nature at present known. The noise of these Falls might be heard an amazing way. I could plainly distinguish them in a calm morning more than twenty miles.

In October 1768 I arrived at Boston, having been absent from it on this expedition two years and five months, and during this time travelled near seven thousand miles. From thence, as soon I had properly digested my Journal and Charts, I set out for England to communicate the discoveries I had made and to render them beneficial to the kingdom. But the prosecution of my plans for reaping these advantages have hitherto been obstructed by the unhappy divisions that have been fomented between Great Britain and the Colonies by their mutual enemies. Should peace once more be restored, I doubt not but that the countries I have described will prove a more abundant source of riches to this nation than either its East or West Indian settlements and I shall not only pride myself, but sincerely rejoice in being the means of pointing out to it so valuable an acquisition.

I cannot conclude the account of my extensive travels without expressing my gratitude to that beneficent Being who invisibly protected me through those perils which unavoidably attended so long a tour among fierce and untutored savages.

At the same time let me not be accused of vanity or presumption if I declare that the motives alleged in the Introduction of this work were not the only ones that induced me to engage in this arduous undertaking. My views were not solely confined to the advantages that might accrue, either to myself or the community to which I belonged, but nobler purposes contributed principally to urge me on.

The confined state, both with regard to civil and religious improvement in which so many of my fellow creatures remained, aroused within my bosom an irresistible inclination to explore the almost unknown regions which they inhabited and, as a preparatory step towards the introduction of more polished manners and more humane sentiments, to gain a knowledge of their language, customs, and principles.

Part Two

OF THE ORIGIN, MANNERS,

CUSTOMS, RELIGION,

AND LANGUAGE

OF THE INDIANS

CHAPTER I

The Origin of the Indians

THE MEANS by which America received its first Inhabitants have, since the time of its discovery by the Europeans, been the subject of numberless disquisitions. Was I to endeavour to collect the different opinions and reasonings of the various writers that have taken up the pen in defence of their conjectures, the enumerations would much exceed the bounds I have prescribed myself, and oblige me to be less explicit on points of greater moment.

From the obscurity in which this debate is enveloped, through the total disuse of letters among every nation of Indians on this extensive continent, and the uncertainty of oral tradition at the distance of so many ages, I fear that even after the most minute investigation, we shall not be able to settle it with any great degree of certainty. And this apprehension will receive additional force when it is considered that the diversity of language, which is apparently distinct between most of the Indians, tends to ascertain that this population was not effected from one particular country but from several neighbouring ones, and completed at different periods.

CHAPTER II

Of the Person and Dress
of the Indians

THE INDIAN nations do not appear to me to differ so widely in their make, colour, or constitution from each other as represented by some writers. They are in general slight made, rather tall and strait, and you seldom see any among them deformed. Their skin is of a reddish or copper colour, their eyes are large and black, and their hair of the same hue, but very rarely is it curled. They have good teeth and their breath is as sweet as the air they draw in; their cheekbones rather raised, but more so in the women than the men. The former are not quite so tall as the European women, however you frequently meet with good faces and agreeable persons among them, although they are more inclined to be fat than the other sex.

Many writers have asserted, that the Indians, even at the maturest period of their existence, are only furnished with hair on their heads and that, notwithstanding the profusion with which that part is covered, those parts which among the inhabitants of other climates are usually the seat of this excrescence remain entirely free from it. But from minute enquiries, and a curious inspection, I am able to declare (however respectable I may hold the authority of these historians in other points) that their assertions are erroneous and proceeding from the want of a thorough knowledge of the customs of the Indians.

After the age puberty, their bodies, in their natural state, are covered in the same manner as those of Europeans. The men, indeed, esteem a beard very unbecoming and take great pains to get rid of it, nor is there any ever to be perceived on their faces, except when they grow old and become inattentive to their appearance. Every crinous efflorescence on the other parts of the body is held unseemly by them, and both sexes employ much time in their extirpation.

The Naudowessies and the remote nations pluck them out with bent pieces of hard wood, formed into a kind of nippers whilst those who have communication with Europeans procure from them wire which they twist into a screw or worm. Applying this to the part, they press the rings together and with a sudden twitch draw out all the hairs that are inclosed between them.

The men of every nation differ in their dress very little from each other, except those who trade with the Europeans. These exchange their furs for blankets, shirts and other apparel which they wear as much for ornament as necessity. The latter fasten by a girdle around their waists about half a yard of broadcloth which covers the middle parts of their bodies. Those who wear shirts never make them fast either at the wrist or collar; this would be a most insufferable confinement to them. They throw their blanket loose upon their shoulders and, holding the upper side of it by the two corners, with a knife in one hand and a tobacco pouch, pipe, &c. in the other, thus accoutred they walk about in their villages or camps. But in their dances they seldom wear this covering.

Those among the men who wish to appear gayer than the rest, pluck from their heads all the hair except a spot on the top of it, about the size of a crown-piece, where it is permitted to grow to a considerable length. On this are fastened plumes of feathers of various colours with silver or ivory quills. The manner of cutting and ornamenting this part of the head distinguishes different nations from each other.

A Man and Woman of the Ottigaumies.

They paint their faces red and black, which they esteem as greatly ornamental. They also paint themselves when they go to war. But the method they make use of on this occasion differs from that wherein they use it merely as a decoration.

The young Indians, who are desirous of excelling their companions in finery, slit the outward rim of both their ears. At the same time they take care not to separate them entirely, but leave the flesh thus cut still untouched at both extremities. Around this spongy substance, from the upper to the lower part, they twist brass wire till the weight draws the amputated rim into a bow of five or six inches diameter, and drags it almost down to the shoulder. This decoration is esteemed to be excessively gay and becoming.

It is also a common custom among them to bore their noses and wear in them pendants of different sorts. I observed that sea shells were much worn by those of the interior parts and reckoned very ornamental. But how they procured them I could not learn—probably by traffick with other nations nearer the sea.

They go without any covering for the thigh except that before spoken of round the middle, which reaches down half way the thighs. But they make for their legs a sort of stocking either of skins or cloth. These are sewed as near to the shape of the leg as possible, so as to admit of being drawn on and off. The edges of the stuff of which they are composed are left annexed to the seam and hang loose for about the breadth of a hand, and this part, which is placed on the outside of the leg, is generally ornamented by those who have any communication with Europeans, if of cloth, with ribands or lace, if of leather, with embroidery and porcupine quills curiously coloured. Strangers who hunt among the Indians in the parts where there is a great deal of snow find these stockings much more convenient than any others.

Their shoes are made of the skin of the deer, elk, or buffalo. These, after being sometimes dressed according to the European manner, at others with the hair remaining on them, are cut into shoes, and fashioned so as to be easy to the feet and convenient for walking. The edges round the ancle are decorated with pieces of brass or tin fixed around leather strings, about an inch long, which being placed very thick make a cheerful tinkling noise either when they walk or dance.

The women wear a covering of some kind or other from the neck to the knees. Those who trade with the Europeans wear a linen garment the same as that used by the men, the flaps of which hang over the petticoat. Such as dress after their ancient manner make a kind of shift with leather which covers the body but not the arms. Their petticoats are made either of leather or cloth, and reach from the waist to the knee. On their legs they wear stockings and shoes, made and ornamented as those of the men.

They differ from each other in the mode of dressing their heads, each following the custom of the nation or band to which they belong and adhering to the form made use of by their ancestors from time immemorial. I remarked that most of the females who dwell on the east side of the Mississippi decorate their heads by inclosing their hair either in ribands, or in plates of silver. The latter is only made use of by the higher ranks, as it is a costly ornament. The silver they use on this occasion is formed into thin plates of about four inches broad, in several of which they confine their hair. That plate which is nearest the head is of considerable width, the next narrower and made so as to pass a little way under the other. In this manner they fasten into each other and, gradually tapering, descend to the waist. The hair of the Indian women being in general very long, this proves an expensive method.

But the women that live to the west of the Mississippi, viz, the Naudowessies, the Assinipoils, &c. divide their hair in the middle of the head, and form it into two rolls, one against each ear. These rolls are about three inches long, and as large as their wrists. They hang in a perpendicular attitude at the front of each ear, and descend as far as the lower part of it.

The women of every nation generally place a spot of paint, about the size of a crown-piece, against each ear. Some of them put paint on their hair and sometimes a small spot in the middle of the forehead.

The Indians, in general, pay a greater attention to their dress and to the ornaments with which they decorate their persons than to the accommodation of their huts or tents. They construct the latter in the following simple and expeditious manner.

Being provided with poles of a proper length, they fasten two of them across near their ends with bands made of bark. Having done this, they raise them up and extend the bottom of each as wide as they purpose to make the area of the tent. They then erect others of an equal height and fix them so as to support the two principal ones. On the whole they lay skins of the elk or deer, sewed together, in quantity sufficient to cover the poles, and by lapping over to form the door. A great number of skins are sometimes required for this purpose, as some of their tents are very capacious. That of the chief warrior of the Naudowessies was at least forty feet in circumference and very commodious.

They observe no regularity in fixing their tents when they encamp, but place them just as it suits their conveniency.

The huts also, which those who use not tents erect when they travel, for very few tribes have fixed abodes or regular towns or villages, are equally simple and almost as soon constructed.

They fix small pliable poles in the ground and bend them till they meet at the top and form a semi-circle, then lash them together. These they cover with mats made of rushes platted, or with birch bark which they carry with them in their canoes for this purpose.

These cabins have neither chimnies nor windows. There is only a small aperture left in the middle of the roofs through which the smoke is discharged, but as this is obliged to be stopped up when it rains or snows violently, the smoke then proves exceedingly troublesome.

They lie on skins, generally those of the bear, which are placed in rows on the ground; and if the floor is not large enough to contain beds sufficient for the accommodation of the whole family, a frame is erected about four or five feet from the ground in which the younger part of it sleep.

As the habitations of the Indians are thus rude, their domestic utensils are few in number and plain in their formation. The tools wherewith they fashion them are so aukward and defective that it is not only impossible to form them with any degree of neatness or elegance, but the time required in the execution is so considerable as to deter them from engaging in the manufacture of such as are not absolutely necessary.

The Naudowessies make the pots in which they boil their victuals of the black clay or stone which resists the effects of the fire nearly as well as iron. When they roast, if it is a large joint or a whole animal such as a beaver, they fix it as Europeans do on a spit made of a hard wood and placing the ends on two forked props, now and then turn it. If the piece is smaller they spit it as before, and fixing the spit in an erect but slanting position, with the meat inclining towards the fire, frequently change the sides till every part is sufficiently roasted.

They make their dishes in which they serve up their meat and their bowls and pans out of the knotty-excrescences of the maple tree or any other wood. They fashion their spoons with a tolerable degree of neatness, as these require much less trouble than larger utensils, from a wood that is termed in America Spoon Wood and which greatly resembles box wood.

Every tribe are now possessed of knives and steels to strike fire with. These being so essentially needful for the common uses of life, those who have not an immediate communication with the European traders purchase them from of such of their neighbours as are situated nearer the settlements, and generally give in exchange for them slaves.

CHAPTER III

Of the Manners and Customs of the Indians

WHEN THE Indian women sit down, they place themselves in a decent attitude, with their knees close together. But from being accustomed to this posture, they walk badly and appear to be lame.

They have no midwives amongst them, their climate or some peculiar happiness in their constitutions rendering any assistance at that time unnecessary. On these occasions they are confined but a few hours from their usual employments, which are commonly very laborious, as the men, who are remarkably indolent, leave to them every kind of drudgery. Even in their hunting parties, the former will not deign to bring home the game, but send their wives for it, though it lies at a very considerable distance.

The women place their children soon after they are born on boards stuffed with soft moss, such as is found in morasses or meadows. The child is laid on its back in one of these kind of cradles and, being wrapped in skins or cloth to keep it warm, is secured in it by small bent pieces of timber.

To these machines they fasten strings by which they hang them to branches of trees; or if they find not trees at hand, fasten them to a stump or stone whilst they transact any needful business. In this position are the children kept for some months. When they are taken out, the boys are suffered to go naked and the girls are covered from the neck to the knees with a shift and a short petticoat.

The Indian women are remarkably decent during their menstrual illness. Those nations that are most remote from the European settlements, as the Naudowessies, &c., are more particularly attentive to this point, though they all without exception adhere to some degree to the same custom.

In every camp or town there is an apartment appropriated for their retirement at this time, to which both single and married retreat, and seclude themselves with the utmost strictness during this period from all society. Afterwards they purify themselves in running streams and return to their different employments.

The men on these occasions most carefully avoid holding any communication with them. The Naudowessies are so rigid in this observance that they will not suffer any belonging to them to fetch such things as are necessary, even fire, from these female lunar retreats, though the want of them is attended with the greatest inconvenience. They are also so superstitious as to think, if a pipe stem cracks, which among them is made of wood, that the possessor has either lighted it at one of these polluted fires or held some converse with a woman during her retirement, which is esteemed by them most disgraceful and wicked.

The Indians are extremely circumspect and deliberate in every word and action. There is nothing that hurries them into any intemperate warmth but that inveteracy to their enemies which is rooted in every Indian heart and never can be eradicated. In all other instances they are cool and remarkably cautious, taking care not to betray on any account whatever their emotions.

If an Indian has discovered that a friend is in danger of being intercepted and cut off by one to whom he has rendered himself obnoxious, he does not inform him in plain and explicit terms of the danger he runs by pursuing the track near which his enemy lies in wait for him, but he first coolly asks him which way he is going that day and, having received his answer, with the same indifference tells him that he has been informed that a dog lies near the spot which might probably do him a mischief. This hint proves sufficient and his friend avoids the danger with as much caution as if every design and motion of his enemy had been pointed out to him.

This apathy often shews itself on occasions that would call forth all the fervour of a susceptible heart. If an Indian has been absent from his family and friends many months, either on a war or hunting party, when his wife and children meet him at some distance from his habitation, instead of the affectionate sensations that would naturally arise in the breast of more refined beings, and productive of mutual congratulations, he continues his course without paying the least attention to those who surround him till he arrives at his home.

He there sits down and, with the same unconcern as if he had not been absent a day, smokes his pipe. Those of his acquaintance who have followed him do the same and perhaps it is several hours before he relates to them the incidents which have befallen him during his absence, though perhaps he has left a father, brother, or son on the field whose loss he ought to have lamented or has been unsuccessful in the undertaking that called him from his home.

Has an Indian been engaged for several days in the chace or on any other laborious expedition, and by accident continued thus long without food, when he arrives at the hut or tent of a friend where he knows his wants may be immediately supplied, he takes care not to show the least symptoms of impatience or to betray the extreme hunger by which he is tortured. But on being invited in, sits contentedly down and smokes his pipe with as much composure as if every appetite was allayed, and he was perfectly at ease. He does the same if among strangers. This custom is strictly adhered to by every tribe, as they esteem it a proof of fortitude and think the reverse would intitle them to the appellation of old women.

If you tell an Indian that his children have greatly signalized themselves against an enemy, have taken many scalps, and brought home many prisoners, he does not appear to feel any extraordinary pleasure on the occasion. His answer generally is, "It is well," and he makes very little further enquiry about it. On the contrary, if you inform him that his children are slain or taken prisoners, he makes no complaints, he only replies, "It does not signify" and probably, for some time at least, asks not how it happened.

This seeming indifference, however, does not proceed from an entire suppression of the natural affections for, notwithstanding they are esteemed savages, I never saw among any other people greater proofs of parental or filial tenderness; and although they meet with their wives after a long absence with the Stoical indifference just mentioned, they are not in general void of conjugal affection.

Another peculiarity is observable in their manner of paying their visits. If an Indian goes to visit a particular person in a family, he mentions to whom his visit is intended and the rest of the family immediately retiring to the other end of the hut or tent are careful not to come near enough to interrupt them during the whole of the conversation. The same method is persued if a man goes to pay his respects to one of the other sex; but then he must be careful not to let love be the subject of his discourse whilst the daylight remains.

The Indians discover an amazing sagacity and acquire with the greatest readiness any thing that depends upon the attention of the mind. By experience and an acute observation, they attain many perfections to which Europeans are strangers. For instance, they will cross a forest or a plain which is two hundred miles in breadth and reach with great exactness the point at which they intend to arrive, keeping during the whole of that space in a direct line, without any material deviations; and this they will do with the same ease whether the weather be fair or cloudy.

With equal acuteness will they point to that part of the heavens the sun is in, though it be intercepted by clouds or fogs. Besides this, they are able to pursue with incredible facility the traces of man or beast, either on leaves or grass; and on this account it is with great difficulty a flying enemy escapes discovery.

They are indebted for these talents not only to nature, but to an extraordinary command of the intellectual faculties which can only be acquired by an unremitted attention and by long experience.

They are in general very happy in a retentive memory; they can recapitulate every particular that has been treated of in council and remember the exact time when these were held. Their belts of wampum preserve the substance of the treaties they have concluded with the neighbouring tribes for ages back, to which they will appeal and refer with as much perspicuity and readiness as Europeans can do to their written records.

Every nation pays great respect to old age. The advice of a father will seldom meet with any extraordinary attention from the young Indians. Probably they receive it with only a bare assent. But they will tremble before a grandfather and submit to his injunctions with the utmost alacrity. The words of the ancient part of their community are esteemed by the young as oracles. If they take during their hunting parties any game that is reckoned by them uncommonly delicious, it is immediately presented to the oldest of their relations.

They never suffer themselves to be overburdened with care, but live in a state of perfect tranquility and contentment. Being naturally indolent, if provision just sufficient for their subsistence can be procured with little trouble and near at hand, they will not go far or take any extraordinary pains for it, though by so doing they might acquire greater plenty and of a more estimable kind.

Having much leisure time they indulge this indolence to which they are so prone by eating, drinking, or sleeping, and rambling about in their towns and camps. But when necessity obliges them to take the field, either to oppose an enemy, or to procure themselves food, they are alert and indefatigable. Many instances of their activity on these occasions will be given when I treat of their wars.

The infatuating spirit of gaming is not confined to Europe; the Indians also feel the bewitching impulse and often lose their arms, their apparel, and every thing they are possessed of. In this case, however, they do not follow the example of more refined gamesters, for they neither murmur nor repine; not a fretful word escapes them, but they bear the frowns of fortune with a philosophic composure.

The greatest blemish in their character is that savage disposition which impels them to treat their enemies with a severity every other nation shudders at. But if they are thus barbarious to those with whom they are war, they are friendly, hospitable, and humane in peace. It may with truth be said of them, that they are the worst enemies, and the best friends of any people in the whole world.

The Indians in general are strangers to the passion of jealousy and brand a man with folly that is distrustful of his wife. Among some bands, the very idea is not known as the most abandoned of their young men very rarely attempt the virtue of married women; nor do these often put themselves in the way of solicitation. Yet the Indian women in general are of an amorous temperament and before they are married are not the less esteemed for the indulgence of their passions.

Whilst I was among the Naudowessies, I observed that they paid uncommon respect to one of their women and found on enquiry that she was intitled to it on account of a transaction that in Europe would have rendered her infamous.

They told me that when she was a young woman, for at the time I saw her she was far advanced in life, she had given what they termed a rice feast. According to an ancient but almost obsolete custom (which, as Hamlet says, would have been more honoured in the breach, than the observance) she invited forty of the principal warriors to her tent where, having feasted them with rice and venison, she by turns regaled each of them with a private desert behind a screen fixed for this purpose in the inner part of the tent.

She had the happiness to obtain by this profusion of courtesy, the favour of her guests and the approbation of the whole band. So sensible were the young Indians of her extraordinary merit that they vied with each other for her hand, and in a very short time one of the principal chiefs took her to wife, over whom she acquired great sway and from whom she received ever after incessant tokens of respect and love.

It is however scarcely once in an age that any females are hardy enough to make this feast, notwithstanding a husband of the first rank awaits as a sure reward the successful giver of it; and the custom, I since find, is peculiar to the Naudowessies.

The Indians, in their common state, are strangers to all distinctions of property, except in the articles of domestic use which every one considers as his own and increase as circumstances admit. They are extremely liberal to each other and supply the deficiency of their friends with any superfluity of their own.

In dangers they readily give assistance to those of their band who stand in need of it without any expectation of return, except of those just rewards that are always conferred by the Indians on merit. Governed by the plain and equitable laws of nature, every one is rewarded solely according to his deserts. Their equality of condition, manners, and privileges, with that constant and sociable familiarity which prevails throughout every Indian nation, animates them with a pure and truly patriotic spirit that tends to the general good of the society to which they belong.

If any of their neighbours are bereaved by death or by an enemy of their children, those who are possessed of the greatest number of slaves supply the deficiency; and these are adopted by them and treated in every respect as if they really were the children of the person to whom they are presented.

The Indians, except those who live adjoining to the European colonies, can form themselves no idea of the value of money. They consider it, when they are made acquainted with the uses to which it is applied by other nations, as the sources of innumerable evils. To it they attribute all the mischiefs that are prevalent among Europeans, such as treachery, plundering, devastations, and murder.

They esteem it irrational that one man should be possessed of a greater quantity than another and are amazed that any honour should be annexed to the possession of it. But that the want of this useless metal should be the cause of depriving persons of their liberty and that on account of this partial distribution of it, great numbers should be immured within the dreary walls of a prison, cut off from that society of which they constitute a part, exceeds their belief. Nor do they fail, on hearing this part of the European system of government related, to charge the institutors of it with a total want of humanity and to brand them with the names of savages and brutes.

They shew almost an equal degree of indifference for the productions of art. When any of these are shewn them, they say, "It is pretty, I like to look at it," but are not inquisitive about the construction of it; neither can they form proper conceptions of its use. But if you tell them of a person who is able to run with great agility, that is well skilled in hunting, can direct with unerring aim a gun, or bend with ease a bow, that can dexterously work a canoe, understands the art of war, is acquainted with the situation of a country, and can make his way without a guide through an immense forest, subsisting during this on a small quantity of provisions, they are in raptures; they listen with great attention to the pleasing tale, and bestow the highest commendations on the hero of it.

CHAPTER IV

The Indian Method
of Reckoning Time

CONSIDERING their ignorance of astronomy, time is very rationally divided by the Indians. Those in the interior parts (and of those I would generally be understood to speak) count their years by winters or, as they express themselves, by snows.

Some nations among them reckon their years by moons and make them consist of twelve synodical or lunar months, observing, when thirty moons have waned, to add a supernumerary one which they term the lost moon, and then begin to count as before. They pay a great regard to the first appearance of every moon and on the occasion always repeat some joyful sounds, stretching at the same time their hands towards it.

Every month has with them a name expressive of its season. For instance, they call the month of March (in which their year generally begins at the first New Moon after the vernal Equinox) the Worm Month or Moon because at this time the worms quit their retreat in the bark of the trees, wood, &c. where they have sheltered themselves during the winter.

The month of April is termed by them the month of Plants. May, the month of flowers. June, the Hot Moon. July, the Buck Moon. Their reason for thus denominating these is obvious.

August, the Sturgeon Moon because in this month they catch great numbers of that fish. September, the Corn Moon because in this month they gather in their Indian corn.

October, the Travelling Moon, as they leave at this time their villages and travel towards the places where they intend to hunt during the winter. November, the Beaver Moon, for in this month the beavers begin to take shelter in their houses, having laid up a sufficient store of provisions for the winter season.

December, the Hunting Moon because they employ this month in pursuit of their game. January, the Cold Moon, as it generally freezes harder and the cold is more intense in this than in any other month. February they call the Snow Moon because more snow commonly falls during this month than any other in the winter.

When the moon does not shine, they say the moon is dead and some call the three last days of it the naked days. The moon's first appearance they term its coming to life again.

They make no division of weeks but days they count by sleeps, half days by pointing to the sun at noon, and quarters by the rising and setting of the sun, to express which they make use of very significant hieroglyphicks.

The Indians are totally unskilled in geography as well as all the other sciences and yet they draw on their birch bark very exact charts or maps of the countries with which they are acquainted. The latitude and longitude is only wanting to make them tolerably complete.

They reckon the distance of places not by miles or leagues but by a day's journey which, according to the best calculations I could make, appears to be about twenty English miles. These they also divide into halves and quarters and will demonstrate them in their maps with great exactness by the hieroglyphicks just mentioned when they regulate in council their war parties or their most distant hunting excursions.

CHAPTER V

Of the Government
of the Indians

EVERY separate body of Indians is divided into bands or tribes, which band or tribe forms a little community with the nation to which it belongs. As the nation has some particular symbol by which it is distinguished from others, so each tribe has a badge from which it is denominated: the Eagle, the Panther, the Tiger, the Buffalo, &c. &c. One band of the Naudowessie is represented by a Snake, another a Tortoise, a third a Squirrel, a fourth a Wolf, and a fifth a Buffalo. Throughout every nation they particularize themselves in the same manner, and the meanest person among them will remember his lineal descent, and distinguish himself by his respective family.

Did not many circumstances tend to confute this supposition, I should be almost induced to conclude from this distinction of tribes, and the particular attachment of the Indians to them, that they derive their origin, as some have asserted, from the Israelites.

Besides this, every nation distinguish themselves by the manner of constructing their tents or huts. And so well versed are all the Indians in this distinction that, though there appears to be no difference on the nicest observation made by an European, yet they will immediately discover from the position of a pole left in the ground what nation has encamped on the spot many months before.

Every band has a chief who is termed a Great Chief or the chief Warrior and who is chosen, in consideration of his experience in war and of his approved valour, to direct their military operations and to regulate all concerns belonging to that department. But this chief is not considered as the head of the state; besides the great warrior, who is elected for his war-like qualifications, there is another who enjoys a pre-eminence as his hereditary right and has the more immediate management of their civil affairs. This chief might with great propriety be denominated the Sachem whose assent is necessary in all conveyances and treaties, to which he affixes the mark of the tribe or nation.

Though these two are considered as the heads of the band, and the latter is usually denominated their king, yet the Indians are sensible of neither civil or military subordination. As every one of them entertains a high opinion of his consequence and is extremely tenacious of his liberty, all injunctions that carry with them the appearance of a positive command, are instantly rejected with scorn.

On this account, it is seldom that their leaders are so indiscreet as to give out any of their orders in a peremptory stile. A bare hint from a chief that he thinks such a thing necessary to be done instantly arouses an emulation among the inferior ranks and is immediately executed with great alacrity. By this method the disgustful part of the command is evaded and an authority that falls little short of absolute sway instituted in its room.

Among the Indians no visible form of government is established; they allow of no such distinction as magistrate and subject, every one appearing to enjoy an independence that cannot be controlled. The object of government among them is rather foreign than domestic, for their attention seems more to be employed in preserving such an union among the members of their tribe as will enable them to watch the motions of their enemies and to act against them with concert and vigour, than to maintain interior order by any public regulations. If a scheme that appears to be of service to the community is proposed by the chief, every one is at liberty to chuse whether he will assist in carrying it on, for they have no compulsory laws that lay them under any restrictions. If violence is committed or blood is shed, the right of revenging these misdemeanours are left to the family of the injured; the chiefs assume neither the power of inflicting or moderating the punishment.

Some nations, where the dignity is hereditary, limit the succession to the female line. On the death of a chief, his sister's son sometimes succeeds him in preference to his own son; and if he happens to have no sister, the nearest female relation assumes the dignity. This accounts for a woman being at the head of the Winnebagoe nation which, before I was acquainted with their laws, appeared strange to me.

Each family has a right to appoint one of its chiefs to be an assistant to the principal chief who watches over the interest of his family, and without whose consent nothing of a public nature can be carried into execution. These are generally chosen for their ability in speaking and such only are permitted to make orations in their councils and general assemblies.

In this body, with the hereditary chief at its head, the supreme authority appears to be lodged, as by its determination every transaction relative to their hunting, to their making war or peace, and to all their public concerns are regulated. Next to these, the body of warriors, which comprehends all that are able to bear arms, hold their rank. This division has sometimes at its head the chief of the nation, if he has signalized himself by any renowned action; if not, some chief that has rendered himself famous.

In their councils which are held by the foregoing members, every affair of consequence is debated and no enterprize of the least moment undertaken unless it there meets with the general approbation of the chiefs. They commonly assemble in a hut or tent appropriate to this purpose and being seated in a circle on the ground, the eldest chief rises and makes a speech. When he has concluded, another gets up, and thus they all speak, if necessary, by turns.

On this occasion their language is nervous, and their manner of expression, emphatical. Their style is adorned with images, comparisons, and strong metaphors, and is equal in allegories to that of any of the eastern nations. In all their set speeches, they express themselves with much vehemence, but in common discourse, according to our usual method of speech.

The young men are suffered to be present at the councils though they are not allowed to make a speech till they are regularly admitted. They however listen with great attention and, to shew that they both understand and approve of the resolutions taken by the assembled chiefs, they frequently exclaim, "That is right." "That is good."

The customary mode among all the ranks expressing their assent and which they repeat at the end of almost every period is by uttering a kind of forcible aspiration, which sounds like an union of the letters OAH.

CHAPTER VI

Of Their Feasts and Dances

MANY OF the Indian nations neither make use of bread, salt or spices and some of them have never seen or tasted of either. The Naudowessies in particular have no bread, nor any substitute for it. They eat the wild rice which grows in great quantities in different parts of their territories, but they boil it and eat it alone. They also eat the flesh of the beasts they kill, without having recourse to any farinaceous substance to absorb the grosser particles of it. And even when they consume the sugar which they have extracted from the maple tree, they use it not to render some other food palatable, but generally eat it by itself.

Neither have they any idea of the use of milk, although they might collect great quantities from the buffalo or the elk; they only consider it as proper for the nutriment of the young of these beasts during their tender state. I could not perceive that any inconveniency attended the total disuse of articles esteemed so necessary and nutritious by other nations; on the contrary, they are in general healthy and vigorous.

One dish however which answers nearly the same purpose as

bread, is in use among the Ottagaumies, the Saukies, and the more eastern nations where Indian corn grows, which is not only more esteemed by them but is reckoned extremely palatable by all the Europeans who enter their dominions. This is composed of their unripe corn as before described, and beans in the same state, boiled together with bear's flesh, the fat of which moistens the pulse and renders it beyond comparison delicious. They call this food Succatosh.

The Indians are far from being cannibals, as they are said to be. All their victuals are either roasted or boiled, and this in the extreme. Their drink is generally the broth in which it has been boiled.

Their food consists of the flesh of the bear, the buffalo, the elk, the deer, the beaver, and the racoon which they prepare in the manner just mentioned. They usually eat the flesh of the deer which is naturally dry with that of the bear which is fat and juicy; and though the latter is extremely rich and luscious, it is never known to cloy.

In the spring of the year the Naudowessies eat the inside bark of a shrub that they gather in some part of their country; but I could neither learn the name of it or discover from whence they got it. It was of a brittle nature and easily masticated. The taste of it was very agreeable, and they said it was extremely nourishing. In flavour it was not unlike the turnip, and when received into the mouth resembled that root both in its pulpous and frangible nature.

The lower ranks of the Indians are exceedingly nasty in dressing their victuals. But some of the chiefs are very neat and cleanly in their apparel, tents, and food.

They commonly eat in large parties, so that their meals may properly be termed feasts; and this they do without being restricted to any fixed or regular hours but just as their appetites require and convenience suits.

They usually dance either before or after every meal and by this cheerfulness probably render the Great Spirit, to whom they consider themselves as indebted for every good, a more acceptable sacrifice than a formal and unanimated thanksgiving. The men and women feast apart and each sex invite by turns their companions to partake with them of the food they happen to have. But in their domestic way of living the men and women eat together.

No people are more hospitable, kind, and free than the Indians. They will readily share with any of their own tribe the last part of their provisions, and even with those of a different nation if they chance to come in when they are eating. Though they do not keep one common stock, yet that community of goods which is so prevalent among them, and their generous disposition, render it nearly of the same effect.

When the chiefs are convened on any public business, they always conclude with a feast at which their festivity and cheerfulness knows no limits.

Dancing is a favourite exercise among the Indians. They never meet on any public occasion but this makes a part of the entertainment. And when they are not engaged in war or hunting, the youth of both sexes amuse themselves in this manner every evening.

They always dance, as I have just observed, at their feasts. In these as well as all their other dances, every man rises in his turn and moves about with great freedom and boldness, singing as he does so the exploits of his ancestors. During this, the company who are seated on the ground in a circle around the dancer join with him in marking the cadence by an odd tone which they utter all together and which sounds, "Heh, heh, heh." These notes, if they might be so termed, are articulated with a harsh accent and strained out with the utmost force of their lungs so that one would imagine their strength must be soon exhausted by it, instead of which they repeat it with the same violence during the whole of their entertainment.

The women, particularly those of the western nations, dance very gracefully. They carry themselves erect and, with their arms hanging down close to their sides, move first a few yards to the right and then back again to the left. This movement they perform without taking any steps as an European would do, but with their feet conjoined, moving by turns their toes and heels. In this manner they glide with great agility to a certain distance and then return. Let those who join in the dance be ever so numerous, they keep time so exactly with each other that no interruption ensues. During this, at stated periods they mingle their shrill voices with the hoarser ones of the men who sit around (for it is to be observed that the sexes never intermix in the same dance) which, with the music of the drums and chichicoues, make an agreeable harmony.

The Indians have several kinds of dances which they use on different occasions, as the Pipe or Calumate Dance, the War Dance, the Marriage Dance, and the Dance of the Sacrifice. The movements in every one of these are dissimilar, but it is almost impossible to convey any idea of the points in which they are unlike.

Different nations likewise vary in their manner of dancing. The Chipeways throw themselves into a greater variety of attitudes than any other people; sometimes they hold their heads erect; at others they bend them almost to the ground, then recline on one side and immediately after on the other. The Naudowessies carry themselves more upright, step firmer, and move more gracefully. But they all accompany their dancers with the disagreeable noise just mentioned.

The Pipe Dance is the principal and the most pleasing to a spectator of any of them, being the least frantic and the movement of it the most graceful. It is but on particular occasions that it is used; as when ambassadors from an enemy arrive to treat of peace or when strangers of eminence pass through their territories.

The War Dance, which they use both before they set out on their war parties and on their return from them, strikes terror into strangers. It is performed, as the others, amidst a circle of warriors. A chief generally begins it, who moves from the right to the left, singing at the same time both his own exploits and those of his ancestors. When he has concluded his account of any memorable action, he gives a violent blow with his war-club against a post that is fixed in the ground near the center of the assembly for this purpose.

Every one dances in his turn and recapitulates the wondrous deeds of his family, till they all at last join in the dance. Then it becomes truly alarming to any stranger that happens to be among them, as they throw themselves into every horrible and terrifying posture that can

A Man & Woman of the Naudowefsie.

139

be imagined, rehearsing at the same time the parts they expect to act against their enemies in the field. During this they hold their sharp knives in their hands, with which, as they whirl about, they are every moment in danger of cutting each others throats; and did they not shun the threatened mischief with inconceivable dexterity, it could not be avoided. By these motions they intend to represent the manner in which they kill, scalp, and take their prisoners. To heighten the scene, they set up the same hideous yells, cries, and war-hoops they use in time of action so that it is impossible to consider them in any other light than as an assembly of demons.

I have frequently joined in this dance with them, but it soon ceased to be an amusement to me, as I could not lay aside my apprehensions of receiving some dreadful wound, that from the violence of their gestures must have proved mortal.

I found that the nations to the westward of the Mississippi and on the borders of Lake Superior still continue to make use of the Paw-waw or Black Dance. The people of the colonies tell a thousand ridiculous stories of the devil being raised in this dance by the Indians. But they allow that this was in former times and is now nearly extinct among those who live adjacent to the European settlements. However I discovered that it was still used in the interior parts and though I did not actually see the devil raised by it, I was witness to some scenes that could be performed by such as dealt with him or were very expert and dextrous jugglers.

I know not under what class of dances to rank that performed by the Indians who came to my tent when I landed near Lake Pepin on the banks of the Mississippi, as related in my Journals. When I looked out, I saw about twenty naked young Indians, the most perfect in their shape and by far the handsomest of any I had ever seen, coming towards me and dancing as they approached to the music of their drums. At every ten or twelve yards they halted and set up their yells and cries.

When they reached my tent, I asked them to come in which, without deigning to make me any answer, they did. As I observed that they were painted red and black, as they usually are when they go against the enemy, and perceived that some parts of the war dance were inter-mixed with their other movements, I doubted not but that they were set on by the inimical chief who had refused my salutation. I therefore determined to sell my life as dear as possible. To this purpose, I received them sitting on my chest, with my gun and pistols beside me, and ordered my men to keep a watchful eye on them and to be also upon their guard.

The Indians being entered, they continued their dance alternately singing at the same time of their heroic exploits and the superiority of their race over every other people. To enforce their language, though it was uncommonly nervous and expressive and such as would of itself have carried terror to the firmest heart, at the end of every period they struck their war-clubs against the poles of my tent, with such violence that I expected every moment it would have tumbled upon us. As each of them, in dancing round, passed by me, they placed their right hands over their eyes and, coming close to me, looked me steadily in the face which I could not construe into a token of friendship. My men gave themselves up for lost and I acknowledge, for my own part, that I never found my apprehensions more tumultuous on any occasion.

When they had nearly ended their dance, I presented to them the pipe of peace, but they would not receive it. I then, as my last resource, thought I would try what presents would do; accordingly I took from my chest some ribands and trinkets which I laid before them. These seemed to stagger their resolutions and to avert in some degree their anger; for after holding a consultation together, they sat down on the ground which I considered as a favourable omen.

Thus it proved, as in a short time they received the pipe of peace and lighting it, first presented it to me and then smoked with it themselves. Soon after they took up the presents which had hitherto lain neglected and, appearing to be greatly pleased with them, departed in a friendly manner. And never did I receive greater pleasure than at getting rid of such formidable guests.

It was not ever in my power to gain a thorough knowledge of the designs of my visiters. I had sufficient reasons to conclude that they were hostile and that their visit, at so late an hour, was made through the instigation of the Grand Sautor. But I was afterwards informed that it might be intended as a compliment which they usually pay to the chiefs of every other nation who happen to fall in with them and that the circumstances in their conduct, which had appeared so suspicious to me, were merely the effects of their vanity and designed to impress on the minds of those whom they thus visited an elevated opinion of their valour and prowess. In the morning before I continued my route, several of their wives brought me a present of some sugar, for whom I found a few more ribands.

CHAPTER VII

Of Their Hunting

HUNTING IS the principal occupation of the Indians; they are trained to it from their earliest youth, and it is an exercise which is esteemed no less honourable than necessary towards their subsistence. A dextrous and resolute hunter is held nearly in as great estimation by them as a distinguished warrior. Scarcely any device which the ingenuity of man has discovered for ensnaring or destroying those animals that supply them with food, or whole skins which are valuable to Europeans, is unknown to them.

Whilst they are engaged on this exercise, they shake off the indolence peculiar to their nature and become active, persevering, and indefatigable. They are equally sagacious in finding their prey and in the means they use to destroy it. They discern the footsteps of the beasts they are in pursuit of, although they are imperceptible to every other eye, and can follow them with certainty through the pathless forest.

The beasts that the Indians hunt, both for their flesh on which they subsist and for their skins, of which they either make their apparel or barter with the Europeans for necessaries, are the buffalo, the elk, the deer, the moose, the carribboo, the bear, the beaver, the otter, the martin, &c. I defer giving a description of these creatures here, and shall only at present treat of their manner of hunting them.

The route they shall take for this purpose, and the parties that shall go on different expeditions, are fixed in their general councils which are held some time in the summer, when all the operations for the ensuing winter are concluded on. The chief-warrior, whose province it is to regulate the proceedings on this occasion, with great solemnity issues out an invitation to those who choose to attend him; for the Indians, as before observed, acknowledge no superiority, nor have they any idea of compulsion, and every one that accepts it prepares himself by fasting during several days.

The Indians do not fast as some other nations do, on the richest and most luxurious food, but they totally abstain from every kind either of victuals or drink; and such is their patience and resolution, that the most extreme thirst could not oblige them to taste a drop of water; yet amidst this severe abstinence they appear cheerful and happy.

The reasons they give for this fasting are that it enables them freely to dream, in which dreams they are informed where they shall find the greatest plenty of game, and also that it averts the displeasure of the evil spirits and induces them to be propitious. They also on these occasions blacken those parts of their bodies that are uncovered.

The fast being ended, and the place of hunting made known, the chief who is to conduct them gives a grand feast to those who are to form the different parties, of which none of them dare to partake till they have bathed themselves. At this feast, notwithstanding they have fasted so long, they eat with great moderation and the chief that presides employs himself in rehearsing the feats of those who have been most successful in the business they are about to enter upon. They soon after set out on the march towards the place appointed, painted or rather bedaubed with black, amidst the acclamations of all the people.

It is impossible to describe their agility or perseverance whilst they are in pursuit of their prey; neither thickets, ditches, torrents, pools, or rivers stop them. They always go straight forward in the most direct line they possibly can and there are few of the savage inhabitants of the woods that they cannot overtake.

When they hunt for bears, they endeavour to find out their retreats; for during the winter, these animals conceal themselves in the hollow trunks of trees or make themselves holes in the ground where they continue without food whilst the severe weather lasts.

When the Indians think they have arrived at a place where these creatures usually haunt, they form themselves into a circle according to their number and moving onward endeavour, as they advance towards the centre, to discover the retreats of their prey. By this means, if any lie in the intermediate space, they are sure of arousing them and bringing them down either with their bows or their guns. The bears will take to flight at sight of a man or a dog and will only make resistance when they are extremely hungry or after they are wounded.

The Indian method of hunting the buffalo is by forming a circle or a square, nearly in the same manner as when they search for the bear. Having taken their different stations, they set the grass, which at this time is rank and dry, on fire and these animals who are extremely fearful of that element, flying with precipitation before it, great numbers are hemmed in a small compass and scarcely a single one escapes.

They have different ways of hunting the elk, deer, and the carribboo. Sometimes they seek them out in the woods, to which they retire during the severity of the cold, where they are easily shot from behind the trees. In the more northern climates, they take the advantage of the weather to destroy the elk. When the sun has just strength enough to melt the snow and the frost in the night forms a kind of crust on the surface, this creature, being heavy, breaks it with his forked hoofs and with difficulty extricates himself from it. At this time therefore he is soon overtaken and destroyed.

Some nations have a method of hunting these animals which is more easily executed and free from danger. The hunting parties divide themselves into two bands and, choosing the spot near the borders of some river, one party embarks on board their canoes whilst the other, forming themselves into a semi-circle on the land, the flanks of which reach the shore, let loose their dogs and by this means rouse all the game that lies within these bounds. They then drive them towards the river, into which they no sooner enter than the greatest part of them are immediately dispatched by those who remain in the canoes.

Both the elk and the buffalo are very furious when they are wounded and will return fiercely on their pursuers and trample them under their feet if the hunter finds not means to complete their destruction or seeks for security in flight to some adjacent tree. By this method they are frequently avoided and so tired with the pursuit that they voluntarily give it over.

But the hunting in which the Indians, particularly those who inhabit the northern parts, chiefly employ themselves and from which they reap the greatest advantage, is the beaver hunting. The season for this is throughout the whole of the winter, from November to April, during which time the fur of these creatures is in the greatest perfection. A description of this extraordinary animal, the construction of their huts, and the regulations of their almost rational community, I shall give in another place.

The hunters make use of several methods to destroy them. Those generally practised are either that of taking them in snares, cutting through the ice, or opening their causeways.

As the eyes of these animals are very quick and their hearing exceedingly acute, great precaution is necessary in approaching their abodes; for as they seldom go far from the water, and their houses are always built close to the side of some large river or lake or dams of their own constructing, upon the least alarm they hasten to the deepest part of the water and dive immediately to the bottom. As they do this they make a great noise by beating the water with their tails, on purpose to put the whole fraternity on their guard.

They take them with snares in the following manner: though the beavers usually lay up a sufficient store of provision to serve for their subsistence during the winter, they make from time to time excursions to the neighbouring woods to procure further supplies of food. The hunters, having found out their haunts, place a trap in their way baited with small pieces of bark or young shoots of trees which the beaver has no sooner laid hold of than a large log of wood falls upon him, and breaks his back. His enemies, who are upon the watch, soon appear and instantly dispatch the helpless animal.

At other times, when the ice on the rivers and lakes is about half a foot thick, they make an opening through it with their hatchets to which the beavers will soon hasten, on being disturbed at their houses, for a supply of fresh air. As their breath occasions a considerable motion in the waters, the hunter has sufficient notice of their approach and methods are easily taken for knocking them on the head the moment they appear above the surface.

When the houses of the beavers happen to be near a rivulet, they are more easily destroyed. The hunters then cut the ice and, spreading a net under it, break down the cabins of the beavers who never fail to make towards the deepest part where they are entangled and taken. But they must not be suffered to remain there long, as they would soon extricate themselves with their teeth which are well known to be exceedingly sharp and strong.

The Indians take great care to hinder their dogs from touching the bones of the beavers. The reasons they give for these precautions are, first that the bones are so excessively hard that they spoil the teeth of the dogs; and, secondly, that they are apprehensive they shall so exasperate the spirits of the beavers by this permission as to render the next hunting season unsuccessful.

The skins of these animals the hunters exchange with the Europeans for necessaries and, as they are more valued by the latter than any other kind of furs, they pay the greatest attention to this species of hunting.

When the Indians destroy buffaloes, elks, deer, &c., they generally divide the flesh of such as they have taken among the tribe to which they belong. But in hunting the beaver, a few families usually unite and divide the spoil between them. Indeed, in the first instance they generally pay some attention in the division to their own families; but no jealousies or murmurings are ever known to arise on account of apparent partiality.

Among the Naudowessies, if a person shoots a deer, buffalo, &c. and it runs to a considerable distance before it drops, where a person belonging to another tribe, being nearer, first sticks a knife into it, the game is considered as the property of the latter, nothwithstanding it had been mortally wounded by the former. Though this custom appears to be arbitrary and unjust, yet that people cheerfully submit to it. This decision is, however, very different from that practiced by the Indians on the back of the colonies where the first person that hits it is entitled to the best share.

CHAPTER VIII

Of Their Manner
of Making War

THE INDIANS begin to bear arms at the age of fifteen, and lay them aside when they arrive at the age of sixty. Some nations to the southward, I have been informed, do not continue their military exercises after they are fifty.

In every band or nation there is a select number who are stiled the Warriors and who are always ready to act either offensively or defensively, as occasion requires. These are well armed, bearing the weapons commonly in use among them which vary according to the situation of their countries. Such as have an intercourse with the Europeans make use of tomahawks, knives, and fire-arms; but those whose dwellings are situated to the westward of the Mississippi and who have not an opportunity of purchasing these kinds of weapons, use bows and arrows and also the Casse Tete or War-club.

The Indians that inhabit still farther to the westward a country which extends to the South Sea use in fight a warlike instrument that is very uncommon. Having great plenty of horses, they always attack their enemies on horseback and encumber themselves with no other weapon than a stone of a middling size, curiously wrought, which they fasten by a string about a yard and half long to their right arms, a little above the elbow. These stones they conveniently carry in their hands till they reach their enemies, and then swinging them with great dexterity as they ride full speed never fail of doing execution. The country which these tribes possess, abounding with large extensive plains, those who attack them seldom return, as the swiftness of the horses on which they are mounted enables them to overtake even the fleetest of their invaders.

The Naudowessies, who had been at war with this people, informed me that unless they found morasses or thickets to which they could retire, they were sure of being cut off. To prevent this they always took care whenever they made an onset, to do it near such retreats as were impassable for cavalry, they then having a great advantage over their enemies whose weapons would not there reach them.

Some nations make use of a javelin pointed with bone worked into different forms. But the Indian weapons in general are bows and arrows and the short club already mentioned. The latter is made of a very hard wood and the head of it fashioned round like a ball about three inches and a half diameter. In this rotund part is fixed an edge resembling that of a tomahawk, either of steel or flint, whichever they can procure.

A dagger in use among the Naudowessie nation was originally made of flint or bone. But since they have had communication with European traders, they have formed it of steel. The length of it is about ten inches and that part close to the handle nearly three inches broad. Its edges are keen and it gradually tapers towards a point. They wear it in a sheath made of deer's leather, neatly ornamented with procupine quills and it is usually hung by a string, decorated in the same manner, which reaches as low only as the breast. This curious weapon is worn by a few of the principal chiefs alone and considered both as an useful instrument and an ornamental badge of superiority.

I observed among the Naudowessies a few targets or shields made of raw buffalo hides, and in the form of those used by the ancients. But as the number of these was small and I could gain no intelligence of the era in which they first were introduced among them, I suppose those I saw had descended from father to son for many generations.

The reasons that the Indians give for making war against one another are much the same as those urged by more civilized nations for disturbing the tranquility of their neighbours. The pleas of the former are however in general more rational and just than such as are brought by Europeans in vindication of their proceedings.

The extension of empire is seldom a motive with these people to invade and to commit depredations on the territories of those who happen to dwell near them. To secure the rights of hunting within particular limits, to maintain the liberty of passing through their accustomed tracks, and to guard those lands which they consider from a long tenure as their own against any infringement are the general causes of those dissensions that so often break out between the Indian nations and which are carried on with so much animosity. Though strangers to the idea of separate property, yet the most uncultivated among them are well acquainted with the rights of their community to the domains they possess, and oppose with vigour every encroachment on them.

Notwithstanding it is generally supposed that from their territories being so extensive, the boundaries of them cannot be ascertained, yet I am well assured that the limits of each nation in the interior parts are laid down in their rude plans with great precision. By theirs, as I have before observed, was I enabled to regulate my own and after the most exact observations and enquiries found very few instances in which they erred.

But interest is not either the most frequent or most powerful incentive to their making war on each other. The passion of revenge, which is the distinguishing characteristic of these people, is the most general motive. Injuries are felt by them with exquisite sensibility, and vengeance pursued with unremitted ardour. To this may be added that natural excitation which every Indian becomes sensible of as soon as he approaches the age of manhood to give proofs of his valour and prowess.

As they are early possessed with a notion that war ought to be the chief business of their lives, that there is nothing more desirous than the reputation of being a great warrior, and that the scalps of their enemies or a number of prisoners are alone to be esteemed valuable, it is not to be wondered at that the younger Indians are continually restless and uneasy if their ardour is repressed and they are kept in a state of inactivity. Either of these propensities, the desire of revenge, or the gratification of an impulse that by degrees becomes habitual to them, is sufficient frequently to induce them to commit hostilities on some of the neighbouring nations.

When the chiefs find any occasion for making war, they endeavour to arouse these habitudes and by that means soon excite their warriors to take arms. To this purpose they make use of their martial eloquence nearly in the following words which never fails of proving effectual: "The bones of our deceased countrymen lie uncovered, they call out to us to revenge their wrongs; and we must satisfy their request. Their spirits cry out against us; they must be appeased. The genii, who are the guardians of our honour, inspire us with a resolution to seek the enemies of our murdered brothers. Let us go and devour those by whom they were slain. Sit therefore no longer inactive; give way to the impulse of your natural valour; anoint your hair; paint your faces; fill your quivers; cause the forests to resound with your songs; console the spirits of the dead; and tell them they shall be revenged."

Animated by these exhortations the warriors snatch their arms in a transport of fury, sing the song of war, and burn with impatience to imbrue their hands in the blood of their enemies.

Sometimes private chiefs assemble small parties and make excursions against those with whom they are at war, or such as have injured them. A single warrior, prompted by revenge or a desire to show his prowess, will march unattended for several hundred miles to surprize and cut off a straggling party.

These irregular sallies, however, are not always approved of by the elder chiefs, though they are often obliged to connive at them, as in the instance before given of the Naudowessie and Chipeway nations.

But when a war is national, and undertaken by the community, their deliberations are formal and slow. The elders assemble in council, to which all the head warriors and young men are admitted, where they deliver their opinions in solemn speeches, weighing with maturity the nature of the enterprize they are about to engage in, and balancing with great sagacity the advantages or inconveniences that will arise from it.

Their priests are also consulted on the subject, and even, sometimes, the advice of the most intelligent of their women is asked.

If the determination be for war, they prepare for it with much ceremony.

The chief warrior of a nation does not on all occasions head the war party himself; he frequently deputes a warrior of whose valour and prudence he has a good opinion. The person thus fixed on, being first bedaubed with black, observes a fast of several days during which he invokes the Great Spirit or deprecates the anger of the evil ones, holding whilst it lasts no converse with any of his tribe.

He is particularly careful at the same time to observe his dreams, for on these do they suppose their success will in a great measure depend; and from the firm persuasion every Indian actuated by his own presumptuous thoughts is impressed with, that he shall march forth to certain victory, these are generally favourable to his wishes.

After he has fasted as long as custom prescribes, he assembles the warriors and holding a belt of wampum in his hand thus addresses them:

"Brothers! by the inspiration of the Great Spirit I now speak unto you, and by him am I prompted to carry into execution the intentions which I am about to disclose to you. The blood of our deceased brothers is not yet wiped away, their bodies are not yet covered, and I am going to perform this duty to them."

Having then made known to them all the motives that induce him to take up arms against the nation with whom they are to engage, he thus proceeds: "I have therefore resolved to march through the warpath to surprize them. We will eat their flesh and drink their blood; we will take scalps, and make prisoners; and should we perish in this glorious enterprize, we shall not be for ever hid in the dust, for this belt shall be a recompence to him who buries the dead." Having said this, he lays the belt on the ground, and he who takes it up declares himself his lieutenant, and is considered as the second in command; this, however, is only done by some distinguished warrior who has a right, by the number of his scalps, to the post.

Though the Indians thus assert that they will eat the flesh and drink the blood of their enemies, the threat is only to be considered as a figurative expression. Notwithstanding they sometimes devour the hearts of those they slay, and drink their blood by way of bravado or to gratify in a more complete manner their revenge, yet they are not naturally anthropophagi, nor ever feed on the flesh of men.

The chief is now washed from his sable covering, anointed with bear's fat, and painted with their red paint in such figures as will make him appear most terrible to his enemies. He then sings the war song and enumerates his warlike actions. Having done this he fixes his eyes on the sun and pays his adorations to the Great Spirit, in which he is accompanied by all the warriors.

This ceremony is followed with dances such as I have before described and the whole concludes with a feast which usually consists of dog's flesh.

This feast is held in the hut or tent of the chief warrior, to which all those who intend to accompany him in his expedition send their dishes to be filled; and during the feast, notwithstanding he has fasted so long, he sits composedly with his pipe in his mouth, and recounts the valorous deeds of his family.

As the hopes of having their wounds, should they receive any, properly treated and expeditiously cured must be some additional inducement to the warriors to expose themselves more freely to danger, the priests, who are also their doctors, prepare such medicines as will prove efficacious. With great ceremony they collect various roots and plants and pretend that they impart to them the power of healing.

Notwithstanding this superstititous method of proceeding, it is very certain that they have acquired a knowledge of many plants and herbs that are of a medicinal quality and which they know how to use with great skill.

From the time the resolution of engaging in a war is taken, to the departure of the warriors, the nights are spent in festivity and their days in making the needful preparations.

If it is thought necessary by the nation going to war to solicit the alliance of any neighbouring tribe, they fix upon one of their chiefs who speaks the language of that people well and who is a good orator and send to them by him a belt of wampum, on which is specified the purport of the embassy in figures that every nation is well acquainted with. At the same time he carries with him a hatchet painted red.

As soon as he reaches the camp or village to which he is destined, he acquaints the chief of the tribe with the general tenor of his commission, who immediately assembles a council to which the ambassador is invited. There, having laid the hatchet on the ground, he holds the belt in his hand and enters more minutely into the occasion of his embassy. In his speech he invites them to take up the hatchet and, as soon as he has finished speaking, delivers the belt.

If his hearers are inclined to become auxiliaries to his nation, a chief steps forward and takes up the hatchet and they immediately espouse with spirit the cause they have thus engaged to support. But if on this application neither the belt or hatchet are accepted, the emissary concludes that the people whose assistance he solicits have already entered into an alliance with the foes of his nation and returns with speed to inform his countrymen of his ill success.

The manner in which the Indians declare war against each other is by sending a slave with a hatchet, the handle of which is painted red, to the nation which they intend to break with; and the messenger, notwithstanding the danger to which he is exposed from the sudden fury of those whom he thus sets at defiance, executes his commission with great fidelity.

Sometimes this token of defiance has such an instantaneous effect on those to whom it is presented that, in the first transports of their fury, a small party will issue forth without waiting for the permission of the elder chiefs and slaying the first of the offending nation they meet, cut open the body and stick a hatchet of the same kind as that they have just received into the heart of their slaughtered foe. Among the more remote tribes this is done with an arrow or spear, the end of which is painted red. And the more to exasperate, they dismember the body to show they esteem them not as men but old women.

The Indians seldom take the field in large bodies, as such numbers would require a greater degree of industry to provide for their subsistence during their tedious marches through dreary forests, or long voyages over lakes and rivers, than they would care to bestow.

Their armies are never encumbered with baggage or military stores. Each warrior, besides his weapons, carries with him only a mat and, whilst at a distance from the frontiers of the enemy, supports himself with the game he kills or the fish he catches.

When they pass through a country where they have no apprehensions of meeting with an enemy, they use very little precaution. Sometimes there are scarcely a dozen warriors left together, the rest being dispersed in pursuit of their game; but though they should have roved to a very considerable distance from the warpath, they are sure to arrive at the place of rendezvous by the hour appointed.

They always pitch their tents long before sun-set and being naturally presumptuous take very little care to guard against a surprize. They place great confidence in their Manitous, or household gods, which they always carry with them. Being persuaded that they take upon them the office of centinels, they sleep very securely under their protection.

These Manitous, as they are called by some nations but are termed Wakons, that is, spirits, by the Naudowessies, are nothing more than otter and martins skins, for which, however, they have a great veneration.

After they have entered the enemies country, no people can be more cautious and circumspect; fires are no longer lighted, no more shouting is heard, nor the game any longer pursued. They are not even permitted to speak but must convey whatever they have to impart to each other by signs and motions.

They now proceed wholly by strategem and ambuscade. Having discovered their enemies, they send to reconnoitre them and a council is immediately held, during which they speak only in whispers, to consider of the intelligence imparted by those who were sent out. The attack is generally made just before day-break, at which period they suppose their foes to be in the soundest sleep. Throughout the whole of the preceding night, they will lie flat upon their faces without stirring and make their approaches in the same posture, creeping upon their hands and feet till they are got within bow-shot of those they have destined to destruction. On a signal given by the chief warrior, to which the whole body makes answer by the most hideous yells, they all start up and, discharging their arrows in the same instant, without giving their adversaries time to recover from the confusion into which they are thrown, pour in upon them with their war-clubs or tomahawks.

The Indians think there is little glory to be acquired from attacking their enemies openly in the field; their greatest pride is to surprize and destroy. They seldom engage without a manifest appearance of advantage. If they find the enemy on their guard, too strongly entrenched, or superior in numbers, they retire, provided there is an opportunity of doing so. And they esteem it the greatest qualification of a chief warrior to be able to manage an attack so as to destroy as many of the enemy as possible at the expense of a few men.

Sometimes they secure themselves behind trees, hillocks, or stones and, having given one or two rounds, retire before they are discovered. Europeans who are unacquainted with this method of fighting too often find to their cost the destructive efficacy of it.

General Braddock was one of this unhappy number. Marching in the year 1755, to attack Fort Du Quesne, he was intercepted by a party of French and confederate Indians in their interest who, by this insidious method of engaging, found means to defeat his army which consisted of about two thousand brave and well-disciplined troops. So securely were the Indians posted, that the English scarcely knew from whence or by whom they were thus annoyed. During the whole of the engagement the latter had scarcely a sight of an enemy and were obliged to retreat without the satisfaction of being able to take the least degree of revenge for the havock made among them. The General paid for this temerity with his life and was accompanied in his fall by a great number of brave fellows whilst his invisible enemies had only two or three of their number wounded.

When the Indians succeed in their silent approaches, and are able to force the camp which they attack, a scene of horror that exceeds description ensues. The savage fierceness of the conquerors and the desperation of the conquered, who well know what they have to expect should they fall alive into the hands of their assailants, occasion the most extraordinary exertions on both sides. The figure of the combatants all besmeared with black and red paint and covered with the blood of the slain, their horrid yells and ungovernable fury, are not to be conceived by those who have never crossed the Atlantic.

Though the Indians are negligent in guarding against surprizes, they are alert and dextrous in surprizing their enemies. To their caution and perseverance in stealing on the party they design to attack, they add that admirable talent or rather instinctive qualification I have already described of tracing out those they are in pursuit of. On the smoothest grass, on the hardest earth, and even on the very stones, will they discover the traces of an enemy, and by the shape of the footsteps, and the distances between the prints, distinguish not only whether it is a man or woman who has passed that way, but even the nation to which they belong. However incredible this might appear, yet, from the many proofs I received whilst among them of their amazing sagacity in this point, I see no reason to discredit even these extraordinary exertions of it.

When they have overcome an enemy, and victory is no longer doubtful, the conquerors first dispatch all such as they think they shall not be able to carry off without great trouble and then endeavour to take as many prisoners as possible. After this they return to scalp those who are either dead or too much wounded to be taken with them.

At this business they are exceedingly expert. They seize the head of the disabled or dead enemy and, placing one of their feet on the neck, twist their left hand in the hair; by this means, having extended the skin that covers the top of the head, they draw out their scalping knives, which are always kept in good order for this cruel purpose, and with a few dextrous strokes take off the part that is termed the scalp. They are so expeditious in doing this that the whole time required scarcely exceeds a minute. These they preserve as monuments of their prowess and at the same time as proofs of the vengeance they have inflicted on their enemies.

If two Indians seize in the same instant a prisoner, and seem to have an equal claim, the contest between them is soon decided; for to put a speedy end to any dispute that might arise, the person that is apprehensive he shall lose his expected reward immediately has recourse to his tomahawk or war-club and knocks on the head the unhappy cause of their contention.

Having completed their purposes, and made as much havock as possible, they immediately retire towards their own country with the spoil they have acquired for fear of being pursued.

Should this be the case, they make use of many strategems to elude the searches of their pursuers. They sometimes scatter leaves, sand, or dust over the prints of their feet; sometimes tread in each others footsteps; and sometimes lift their feet so high and tread so lightly as not to make any impression on the ground. But if they find all these precautions unavailing, and that they are near being overtaken, they first dispatch and scalp their prisoners and then dividing, each endeavours to regain his native country by a different route. This prevents all farther pursuit, for their pursuers now despairing, either of gratifying their revenge, or of releasing those of their friends who were made captives, return home.

If the succesful party is so lucky as to make good their retreat unmolested, they hasten with the greatest expedition to reach a country where they may be perfectly secure, and that their wounded companions may not retard their flight, they carry them by turns in litters or, if it is the winter season, draw them on sledges.

Their litters are made in a rude manner of the branches of trees. Their sledges consist of two small thin boards about a foot wide when joined, and near six feet long. The fore part is turned up and the sides are bordered with small bands. The Indians draw these carriages with great ease, be they ever so much loaded, by means of a string which passes round the breast. This collar is called a Metump and is in use throughout America, both in the settlements and the internal parts. Those used in the latter are made of leather and very curiously wrought.

The prisoners during their march are guarded with the greatest care. During the day, if the journey is over land, they are always held by some of the victorious party; if by water, they are fastened to the canoe. In the night-time, they are stretched along the ground quite naked, with their legs, arms, and neck fastened to hooks fixed in the ground. Besides this, cords are tied to their arms or legs, which are held by an Indian who instantly awakes at the least motion of them.

Notwithstanding such precautions are usually taken by the Indians, it is recorded in the annals of New England that one of the weaker sex, almost alone and unassisted, found means to elude the vigilance of a party of warriors, and not only to make her escape from them, but to revenge the cause of her countrymen.

Some years ago, a small band of Canadian Indians, consisting of ten warriors attended by two of their wives, made an irruption into the back settlements of New England. They lurked for some time in the vicinity of one of the most exterior towns and, at length, after having killed and scalped several people, found means to take prisoner a woman who had with her a son of about twelve years of age. Being satisfied with the execution they had done, they retreated towards their native country which lay at three hunded miles distance, and carried off with them their two captives.

The second night of their retreat, the woman, whose name, if I mistake not, was Rowe, formed a resolution worthy of the most intrepid hero. She thought she should be able to get from her hands the manacles by which they were confined, and determined if she did so to make a desperate effort for the recovery of her freedom. To this purpose, when she concluded that her conquerors were in their soundest sleep, she strove to slip the cords from her hands. In this she succeeded and cautioning her son, whom they had suffered to go unbound, in a whisper against being surprized at what she was about to do, she removed to a distance with great wariness the defensive weapons of the Indians, which lay by their sides.

Having done this, she put one of the tomahawks into the hands of the boy, bidding him to follow her example and, taking another herself, fell upon the sleeping Indians, several of whom she instantly dispatched. But her attempt was nearly frustrated by the imbecility of her son who, wanting both strength and resolution, made a feeble stroke at one of them, which only served to awaken him. She however sprung at the rising warrior and, before he could recover his arms, made him sink under the weight of her tomahawk; and this she alternately did to all the rest, except one of the women who awoke in time and made her escape.

The heroine then took off the scalps of her vanquished enemies and, seizing also those they were carrying away with them as proofs of their success, she returned in triumph to the town from whence she had so lately been dragged, to the great astonishment of her neighbours who could scarcely credit their senses or the testimonies she bore of her Amazonian intrepidity.

During their march they oblige their prisoners to sing their death-song, which generally consists of these or similar sentences: "I am going to die, I am about to suffer but I will bear the severest tortures my enemies can inflict with becoming fortitude. I will die like a brave man and I shall then go to join the chiefs that have suffered on the same account." These songs are continued with necessary intervals, until they reach the village or camp to which they are going.

When the warriors are arrived within hearing, they set up different cries which communicates to their friends a general history of the success of the expedition. The number of the death-cries they give declares how many of their own party are lost; the number of war-hoops, the number of prisoners they have taken.

It is difficult to describe these cries, but the best idea I can convey of them is that the former consists of the sound Whoo, Whoo, Whoop, which is continued in a long shrill tone nearly till the breath is exhausted and then broken off with a sudden elevation of the voice.

The latter of a loud cry, of much the same kind, which is modulated into notes by the hand being placed before the mouth. Both of them might be heard to a very considerable distance.

Whilst these are uttering, the persons to whom they are designed to convey the intelligence continue motionless and all attention. When this ceremony is performed, the whole village issue out to learn the particulars of the relation they have just heard in general terms and, according as the news prove mournful or the contrary, they answer by so many acclamations or cries of lamentation.

Being by this time arrived at the village or camp, the women and children arm themselves with sticks and bludgeons and form themselves into two ranks through which the prisoners are obliged to pass. The treatment they undergo before they reach the extremity of the line is very severe. Sometimes they are so beaten over the head and face as to have scarcely any remains of life and happy would it be for them if by this usage an end was put to their wretched beings. But their tormentors take care that none of the blows they give prove mortal, as they wish to reserve the miserable sufferers for more severe inflictions.

After having undergone this introductory discipline, they are bound hand and foot whilst the chiefs hold a council in which their fate is determined. Those who are decreed to be put to death by the usual torments are delivered to the chief of the warriors; such as are to be spared are given into the hands of the chief of the nation, so that in a short time all the prisoners may be assured of their fate, as the sentence now pronounced is irrevocable. The former they term being consigned to the house of death, the latter to the house of grace.

Such captives as are pretty far advanced in life, and have acquired great honour by their warlike deeds, always atone for the blood they have spilt by the tortures of fire. Their success in war is readily known by the blue marks upon their breasts and arms which are as legible to the Indians as letters are to Europeans.

The manner in which these hieroglyphicks are made is by breaking the skin with the teeth of fish or sharpened splints, dipped in a kind of ink made of the soot of pitch pine. Like those of the ancient

Picts of Britain, these are esteemed ornamental; and at the same time they serve as registers of the heroic actions of the warrior who thus bears about him indelible marks of his valour.

The prisoners destined to death are soon led to the place of execution, which is generally in the center of the camp or village where, being stript and every part of their bodies blackened, the skin of a crow or raven is fixed on their heads. They are then bound to a stake with faggots heaped around them and obliged for the last time to sing their death-song.

The warriors, for such it is only who commonly suffer this punishment, now perform in a more prolix manner this sad solemnity. They recount with an audible voice all the brave actions they have performed and pride themselves in the number of enemies they have killed. In this rehearsal they spare not even their tormentors, but strive by every provoking tale they can invent to irritate and insult them. Sometimes this has the desired effect and the sufferers are dispatched sooner than they otherwise would have been.

There are many other methods which the Indians make use of to put their prisoners to death, but these are only occasional. That of burning is most generally used.

Whilst I was at the chief town of the Ottagaumies, an Illinois Indian was brought in who had been made prisoner by one of their war parties. I had then an opportunity of seeing the customary cruelties inflicted by these people on their captives through the minutest part of their process. After the previous steps necessary to his condemnation, he was carried early in the morning to a little distance from the town where he was bound to a tree.

This being done, all the boys, who amounted to a great number as the place was populous, were permitted to amuse themselves with shooting their arrows at the unhappy victim. As they were none of them more than twelve years old and were placed a considerable distance, they had not strength to penetrate to the vital parts, so that the poor wretch stood pierced with arrows and suffering the consequent agonies, for more than two days.

During this time he sung his warlike exploits. He recapitulated every stratagem he had made use of to surprize his enemies. He boasted of the quantity of scalps he possessed and enumerated the prisoners he had taken. He then described the different barbarous methods by which he had put the latter to death and seemed even then to receive inconceivable pleasure from the recital of the horrid tale.

But he dwelt more particularly on the cruelties he had practiced on such of the kindred of his present tormentors as had fallen into his hands, endeavouring by these aggravated insults to induce them to increase his tortures, that he might be able to give greater proofs of fortitude. Even in the last struggles of life, when he was no longer able to vent in words the indignant provocation his tongue would have uttered, a smile of mingled scorn and triumph sat on his countenance.

This method of tormenting their enemies is considered by the Indians as productive of more than one beneficial consequence. It satiates in a greater degree that diabolical passion in the breast of every individual of every tribe, and it gives the growing warriors an early propensity to that cruelty and thirst for blood which is so necessary a qualification for such as would be thoroughly skilled in their savage art of war.

I have been informed that an Indian who was under the hands of his tormentors had the audacity to tell them that they were ignorant old women and did not know how to put brave prisoners to death. He acquainted them that he had heretofore taken some of their warriors and instead of the trivial punishments they inflicted on him, he had devised for them the most excruciating torments, that having bound them to a stake, he had stuck their bodies full of sharp splinters of turpentine wood to which he then set fire and dancing around them enjoyed the agonizing pangs of the flaming victims.

This bravado, which carried with it a degree of insult that even the accustomed ear of an Indian could not listen to unmoved, threw his tormentors off their guard and shortened the duration of his torments, for one of the chiefs ran to him and, ripping out his heart, stopped with it the mouth from which had issued such provoking language.

Innumerable are the stories that may be told of the courage and resolution of the Indians who happen to be made prisoners of their adversaries. Many that I have heard are so astonishing that they seem to exceed the utmost limits of credibility; it is, however, certain that these savages are possessed with many heroic qualities and bear every species of misfortune with a degree of fortitude which has not been outdone by any of the ancient heroes of either Greece or Rome.

Notwithstanding these acts of severity exercised by the Indians towards those of their own species who fall into their hands, some tribes of them have been remarked for their moderation to such female prisoners belonging to the English colonies as have happened to be taken by them. Women of great beauty have frequently been carried off by them and, during a march of three or four hundred miles through their forests, have lain by their sides without receiving any insult and their chastity has remained inviolate. Instances have happened where female captives, who have been pregnant at the time of their being taken, have found the pangs of child-birth come upon them in the midst of solitary woods, and savages their only companions; yet from these, savages as they were, have they received every assistance their situation would admit of, and been treated with a degree of delicacy and humanity they little expected.

This forebearance, it must be acknowledged, does not proceed altogether from their dispositions but is only inherent in those who have held some communication with the French missionaries. Without intending that their natural enemies, the English, should enjoy the benefit of their labours, these fathers have taken great pains to inculcate on the minds of the Indians the general principles of humanity which has diffused through their manners and has proved of public utility.

Those prisoners that are consigned to the house of grace, and these are commonly the young men, women, and children, await the disposal of the chiefs who, after the execution of such as are condemned to die, hold a council for this purpose.

A herald is sent round the village or camp to give notice that such as have lost any relation in the late expedition are desired to attend the distribution which is about to take place. Those women who have lost their sons or husbands are generally satisfied in the first place; after these, such as have been deprived of friends of a more remote degree of consanguinity, or who choose to adopt some of the youth.

The division being made, which is done as in other cases without the least dispute, those who have received any share lead them to their tents or huts and, having unbound them, wash and dress their wounds if they happen to have received any. They then cloath them and give them the most comfortable and refreshing food their store will afford.

Whilst their new domesticks are feeding, they endeavour to administer consolation to them. They tell them that as they are redeemed from death, they must now be cheerful and happy and if they serve them well, without murmuring or repining, nothing shall be wanting to make them such atonement for the loss of their country and friends as circumstances will allow of.

If any men are spared, they are commonly given to the widows that have lost their husbands by the hand of the enemy, should there be any such, to whom, if they happen to prove agreeable, they are soon married. But should the dame be otherwise engaged, the life of him who falls to her lot is in great danger; especially if she fancies that her late husband wants a slave in the country of spirits to which he is gone.

When this is the case, a number of young men take the devoted captive to some distance and dispatch him without any ceremony. After he has been spared by the council, they consider him of too little consequence to be intitled to the torments allotted to those who have been judged worthy of them.

The women are usually distributed to the men, from whom they do not fail of meeting with a favourable reception. The boys and girls are taken into the families of such as have need of them, and considered as slaves and it is not uncommon that they are sold in the same capacity to the European traders who come among them.

The Indians have no idea of moderating the ravages of war by sparing their prisoners and entering into a negotiation with the band from whom they have been taken for an exchange. All that are captivated by both parties are either put to death, adopted, or made slaves of. And so particular are every nation in this respect that if any of their tribe, even a warrior, should be taken prisoner and by chance be received into the house of grace, either as an adopted person or a slave, and should afterwards make his escape, they will by no means receive him, or acknowledge him as one of their band.

The condition of such as are adopted differs not in any one instance from the children of the nation to which they now belong. They assume all the rights of those whose places they supply and frequently make no difficulty of going in the war-parties against their own countrymen. Should, however, any of these by chance make their escape and be afterwards retaken, they are esteemed as unnatural children and ungrateful persons who have deserted and made war upon their parents and benefactors and are treated with uncommon severity.

That part of the prisoners which are considered as slaves are generally distributed among the chiefs who frequently make presents of some of them to the European governors of the out-posts or to the superintendants or commissaries of Indian affairs. I have been informed that it was the Jesuits and French missionaries that first occasioned the introduction of these unhappy captives into the settlements and who by so doing taught the Indian that they were valuable.

Their views indeed were laudable, as they imagined that by this method they should not only prevent much barbarity and bloodshed, but find the opportunities of spreading their religion among them increased. To this purpose they encouraged the traders to purchase such slaves as they met with.

The good effects of this mode of proceeding was not however equal to the expectations of these pious fathers. Instead of being the means of preventing cruelty and bloodshed, it only caused the dissensions between the Indian nations to be carried on with a greater degree of violence and with unremitted ardour. The prize they fought for being no longer revenge or fame, but the acquirement of spirituous liquors for which their captives were to be exchanged, and of which almost every nation is immoderately fond, they fought their enemies with unwonted alacrity, and were constantly on the watch to surprize and carry them off.

It might still be said that fewer of the captives are tormented and put to death since these expectations of receiving so valuable a consideration for them have been excited than there usually had been; but it does not appear that their accustomed cruelty to the warriors they take is in the least abated; their natural desire of vengeance must be gratified; they now only become more assiduous in securing a greater number of young prisoners, whilst those who are made captive in their defence are tormented and put to death as before.

The missionaries, finding that contrary to their wishes their zeal had only served to increase the sale of the noxious juices, applied to the Governor of Canada in the year 1693 for a prohibition of this baneful trade. An order was issued accordingly, but it could not put a total stop to it; the French Couriers de Bois were hardy enough to carry it on clandestinely, notwithstanding the penalty annexed to a breach of the prohibition was a considerable fine and imprisonment.

Some who were detected in the prosecution of it withdrew into the Indian countries where they intermarried with the natives and underwent a voluntary banishment. These, however, being an abandoned and debauched set, their conduct contributed very little either towards reforming the manners of their new relations or engaging them to entertain a favourable opinion of the religion they professed. Thus did these indefatigable religious men see their designs in some measure once more frustrated.

The Indians consider every conquered people as in a state of vassalage to their conquerors. After one nation has finally subdued another, and a conditional submission is agreed on, it is customary for the chiefs of the conquered, when they sit in council with their subduers, to wear petticoats, as an acknowledgment that they are in a state of subjection, and ought to be ranked among the women.

CHAPTER IX

Of Their Manner
of Making Peace

THE WARS that are carried on between the Indian nations are in general hereditary, and continue from age to age with a few interruptions. If a peace becomes necessary, the principal care of both parties is to avoid the appearance of making the first advances.

When they treat with an enemy, relative to a suspension of hostilities, the chief who is commissioned to undertake the negotiation, if it is not brought about by the mediation of some neighbouring band, abates nothing of his natural haughtiness. Even when the affairs of his country are in the worst situation, he makes no concessions, but endeavours to persuade his adversaries that it is in their interest to put an end to the war.

Accidents sometimes contribute to bring about a peace between nations that otherwise could not be prevailed on to listen to terms of accommodation. An instance of this, which I heard of in almost every nation I passed through, I shall relate.

About eighty years ago, the Iroquois and Chipeways, two powerful nations, were at war with the Ottagaumies and Saukies, who were much inferior to their adversaries both in numbers and strength. One winter near a thousand of the former made an excursion from Lake Ontario, by way of Toronto, towards the territories of their enemies. They coasted Lake Huron on its east and northern borders till they arrived at the island of St. Joseph, which is situated in the Straits of St. Marie. There they crossed these Straits upon the ice about fifteen miles below the falls and continued their route still westward. As the ground was covered with snow, to prevent a discovery of their numbers they marched in single file, treading in each others footsteps.

Four Chipeway Indians, passing that way, observed this army and readily guessed from the direction of their march, and the precautions they took, both the country to which they were hastening, and their designs.

Notwithstanding the nation to which they belonged was at war with the Ottagaumies, and in alliance with their invaders, yet from a principle which cannot be accounted for, they took an instant resolution to apprize the former of their danger. To this purpose they hastened away with their usual celerity and, taking a circuit to avoid discovery, arrived at the hunting grounds of the Ottagaumies before so large a body, moving in so cautious a manner, could do. There they found a party of about four hundred warriors, some of which were Saukies, whom they informed of the approach of their enemies.

The chiefs immediately collected their whole force and held a council on the steps that were to be taken for their defence. As they were encumbered with their families, it was impossible that they could retreat in time; they therefore determined to chuse the most advantageous spot and to give the Iroquois the best reception in their power.

Not far from the place where they then happened to be, stood two small lakes, between which ran a narrow neck of land about a mile in length and only from twenty to forty yards in breadth. Concluding that the Iroquois intended to pass through this defile, the united bands divided their little party into two bodies of two hundred each. One of these took post at the extremity of the pass that lay nearest to their hunting grounds, which they immediately fortified with a breast-work formed of palisades, whilst the other body took a compass round one of the lakes, with a design to hem their enemies in when they had entered the defile.

Their strategem succeeded; for no sooner had the whole of the Iroquois entered the pass than, being provided with wood for the purpose, they formed a similar breast-work on the other extremity, and thus enclosed their enemies.

The Iroquois soon perceived their situation, and immediately held a council on the measures that were necessary to be pursued to extricate themselves. Unluckily for them a thaw had just taken place which had so far dissolved the ice as to render it impassible, and yet there still remained sufficient to prevent them from either passing over the lakes on rafts, or from swimming across. In this dilemma it was agreed that they should endeavour to force one of the breast-works; but they soon found them too well defended to effect their purpose.

Notwithstanding their disappointment, with the usual composure and unapprehensiveness of Indians, they amused themselves three or four days in fishing. By this time the ice being quite dissolved, they made themselves rafts, which they were enabled to do by some trees that fortunately grew on the spot, and attempted to cross one of the lakes.

They accordingly set off before daybreak. But the Ottagaumies, who had been watchful of their motions, perceiving their design, detached one hundred and fifty men from each of their parties to oppose their landing. These three hundred marched so expeditiously to the other side of the lake that they reached it before their opponents had gained the shore, they being retarded by their poles sticking in the mud.

As soon as the confederates arrived, they poured in a very heavy fire, both from their bows and musquetry, on the Iroquois, which greatly disconcerted them till the latter finding their situation desperate, leaped into the water and fought their way through their enemies. This however they could not do without losing more than half their men.

After the Iroquois had landed, they made good their retreat, but were obliged to leave their enemies masters of the field and in possession of all the furs they had taken during their winter's hunt. Thus dearly did they pay for an unprovoked excursion to such distance from the route they ought to have pursued, and to which they were only impelled by a sudden desire of cutting off some of their ancient enemies.

But had they known their strength they might have destroyed every man of the party that opposed them which, even at the first onset, was only inconsiderable and, when diminished by the action, totally unable to make any stand against them.

The victorious bands rewarded the Chipeways, who had been the means of their success, with a share of the spoils. They pressed them to take any quantity they chose of the richest of the furs and sent them under an escort of fifty men to their own country. The disinterested Chipeways, as the Indians in general are seldom actuated by mercenary motives, for a considerable time refused these presents, but were at length persuaded to accept of them.

The brave and well-concerted resistance here made by the Ottagaumies and Saukies, aided by the mediation of the Chipeways who, laying aside on this occasion the animosity they had so long borne those people approved of the generous conduct of their four chiefs, were together the means of effecting a reconciliation between these nations; and, in process of time, united them all in the bands of amity.

And I believe that all the Indians inhabiting that extensive country which lies between Quebec, the banks of the Mississippi north of the Ouisconsin, and the settlements belonging to the Hudson's Bay Company are at present in a state of profound peace. When their restless dispositions will not suffer them to remain inactive, these northern Indians seldom commit hostilities on each other, but make excursions to the southward against the Cherokees, Choctahs, Chickasaws or Illinois.

Sometimes the Indians grow tired of a war which they have carried on against some neighbouring nation for many years without much success, and in this case they seek for mediators to begin a negotiation. These being obtained, the treaty is thus conducted.

A number of their own chiefs, joined by those who have accepted the friendly office, set out together for the country of their enemies. Such as are chosen for this purpose are chiefs of the most extensive abilities and of the greatest integrity. They bear before them the Pipe of Peace, which I need not inform my readers is of the same nature as a Flag of Truce among the Europeans, and is treated with the greatest respect and veneration, even by the most barbarous nations. I never heard of an instance wherein the bearers of this sacred badge of friendship were ever treated disrespectfully, or its rights violated. The Indians believe that the Great Spirit never suffers an infraction of this kind to go unpunished.

The Pipe of Peace, which is termed by the French the Calumet, for what reason I could never learn, is about four feet long. The bowl of it is made of red marble, and the stem of it of a light wood, curiously painted with hieroglyphicks in various colours and adorned with the feathers of the most beautiful birds. It is not in my power to convey an idea of the various tints and pleasing ornaments of this much esteemed Indian implement.

Every nation has a different method of decorating these pipes, and they can tell at first sight to what band it belongs. It is used as an introduction to all treaties, and great ceremony attends the use of it on these occasions.

The assistant or aid-du-camp of the great warrior, when the chiefs are assembled and seated, fills it with tobacco mixed with herbs, taking care at the same time that no part of it touches the ground. When it is filled, he takes a coal that is thoroughly kindled from a fire which is generally kept burning in the midst of the assembly, and places it on the tobacco.

As soon as it is sufficiently lighted, he throws off the coal. He then turns the stem of it towards the heavens, after this towards the earth and, now holding it horizontally, moves himself round till he has completed a circle. By the first action he is supposed to present it to the Great Spirit, whose aid is thereby supplicated; by the second, to avert any malicious interposition of the evil spirits; and by the third to gain the protection of the spirits inhabiting the air, the earth, and the waters. Having thus secured the favour of those invisible agents, in whose power they suppose it is either to forward or obstruct the issue of their present deliberations, he presents it to the hereditary chief who, having taken two or three whiffs, blows the smoke from his mouth first towards heaven, and then around him upon the ground.

It is afterwards put in the same manner into the mouths of the ambassadors or strangers who observe the same ceremony; then to the chiefs of the warriors and to all the other chiefs in turn according to their gradation. During this time the person who executes this honourable office holds the pipe slightly in his hand, as if he feared to press the sacred instrument; nor does any one presume to touch it but with his lips.

When the chiefs who are instructed with the commission for making peace approach the town or camp to which they are going, they begin to sing and dance the songs and dances appropriated to this occasion. By this time the adverse party are apprized of their arrival and, divesting themselves of their wonted enmity at the sight of the Pipe of Peace, invite them to the habitation of the Great Chief and furnish them with every conveniency during the negotiation.

A council is then held and when the speeches and debates are ended, if no obstructions arise to put a stop to the treaty, the painted hatchet is buried in the ground as a memorial that all animosities between the contending nations have ceased, and a peace taken place. Among the ruder bands, such as have no communication with the Europeans, a war-club painted red is buried instead of the hatchet.

A belt of wampum is also given on this occasion, which serves as a ratification of the peace and records to the latest posterity, by the hieroglyphicks into which the beads are formed, every stipulated article on the treaty.

These belts are made of shells found on the coasts of New England and Virginia, which are sawed out into beads of an oblong form, about a quarter of an inch long and round like other beads. Being strung on leather strings, and several of them sewed neatly together

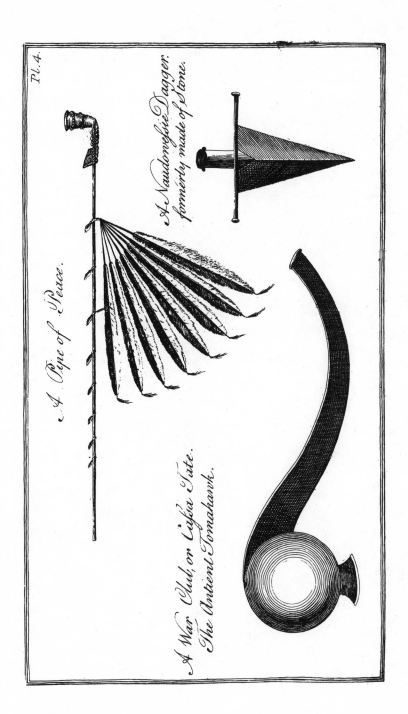

Pl. 4.

A Naudowessie Dagger, formerly made of Stone.

A Pipe of Peace.

A War Club, or Cassa Tate. The Antient Tomahawk.

with fine sinewy threads, they then compose what is termed a belt of wampum.

The shells are generally of two colours, some white and others violet; but the latter are more highly esteemed than the former. They are held in as much estimation by the Indians as gold, silver, or precious stones are by the Europeans.

The belts are composed of ten, twelve, or a greater number of strings, according to the importance of the affair in agitation, or the dignity of the person to whom it is presented. On more trifling occasions, strings of these beads are presented by the chiefs to each other, and frequently worn by them about their necks as a valuable ornament.

CHAPTER X

Of Their Games

THE INDIANS are greatly addicted to gaming, and will even stake, and lose with composure, all the valuables they are possessed of. They amuse themselves at several sorts of games, but the principal and most esteemed among them is that of the ball, which is not unlike the European game of tennis.

The balls they use are rather larger than those made use of at tennis and are formed of a piece of deer-skin which, being moistened to render it supple, is stuffed hard with the hair of the same creature and sewed with its sinews. The ball-sticks are about three feet long, at the end of which there is fixed a kind of racket, resembling the palm of the hand and fashioned of things cut from a deer-skin. In these they catch the ball and throw it to a great distance, if they are not prevented by some of the opposite party who fly to intercept it.

They begin by fixing two poles in the ground at about six hundred yards apart, and one of these goals belongs to each party of the combatants. The ball is thrown up high in the centre of the ground and in a direct line between the goals towards which each party endeavours to strike it, and which ever side first causes it to reach their own goal reckons towards the game.

They are so exceeding dextrous in this manly exercise that the ball is usually kept flying in different directions by the force of the rackets, without touching the ground during the whole contention; for they are not allowed to catch it with their hands. They run with amazing velocity in pursuit of each other and, when one is on the point of hurling it to a great distance, an antagonist overtakes him, and by a sudden stroke dashes down the ball.

They play with so much vehemence that they frequently wound each other, and sometimes a bone is broken; but notwithstanding these accidents there never appears to be any spite or wanton exertions of strength to effect them, nor do any disputes ever happen between the parties.

There is another game also in use among them worthy of remark, and this is the game of the Bowl or Platter. This game is played between two persons only. Each person has six or eight little bones not unlike a peach-stone either in size or shape, except that they are quadrangular, two of the sides of which are coloured black and the others white. These they throw up into the air, from whence they fall into a bowl or platter placed underneath and made to spin round.

According as these bones present the white or black side upwards they reckon the game: he that happens to have the greatest number turn up of a similar colour, counts five points; and forty is the game.

The winning party keeps his place, and the loser yields his to another who is appointed by one of the umpires; for a whole village is sometimes concerned in the party and at times one band plays against another.

During this play the Indians appear to be greatly agitated, and at every decisive throw set up a hideous shout. They make a thousand contortions, addressing themselves at the same time to the bones, and loading with imprecations the evil spirits that assist their successful antagonists. At this game some will lose their apparel, all the moveables of their cabins, and sometimes even their liberty, notwithstanding there are no people in the universe more jealous of the latter than the Indians are.

CHAPTER XI

Of Their Marriage Ceremonies

T HE INDIANS allow of polygamy and persons of every rank
indulge themselves in this point. The chiefs in particular have a
seraglio which consists of an uncertain number, usually from six to
twelve or fourteen. The lower ranks are permitted to take as many as
there is a probability of their being able, with the children they bear,
to maintain. It is not uncommon for an Indian to marry two sisters;
sometimes, if there happen to be more, the whole number; and
notwithstanding this (as it appears to civilized nations) unnatural
union, they all live in the greatest harmony.

The younger wives are submissive to the elder; and those who have
no children, do such menial offices for those who are fertile as causes
their situation to differ but little from a state of servitude. However
they perform every injunction with the greatest cheerfulness in hopes
of gaining thereby the affection of their husband, that they in their
turns may have the happiness of becoming mothers and be intitled to
the respect attendant on that state.

It is not uncommon for an Indian, although he takes to himself so many wives, to live in a state of continence with many of them for several years. Such as are not so fortunate as to gain the favour of their husband by their submissive and prudent behaviour, and by that means to share in his embraces, continue in their virgin state during the whole of their lives, except they happen to be presented by him to some stranger chief whose abode among them will not admit of his entering into a more lasting connection. In this case they submit to the injunction of their husband without murmuring and are not displeased at the temporary union. But if at any time it is known that they take this liberty without first receiving his consent, they are punished in the same manner if they had been guilty of adultery.

This custom is more prevalent among the nations which lie in the interior parts than among those that are nearer the settlements, as the manners of the latter are rendered more conformable in some points to those of the Europeans, by the intercourse they hold with them.

The Indian nations differ but little from each other in their marriage ceremonies, and less in the manner of their divorces. The tribes that inhabit the borders of Canada, make use of the following custom.

When a young Indian has fixed his inclinations on one of the other sex, he endeavours to gain her consent, and if he succeeds, it is never known that her parents ever obstruct their union. When every preliminary is agreed on, and the day appointed, the friends and acquaintances of both parties assemble at the house or tent of the oldest relation of the bridegroom, where a feast is prepared on the occasion.

The company who meet to assist at the festival are sometimes very numerous; they dance, they sing, and enter into every other diversion usually made use of on any of their public rejoicings. When these are finished, all those who attended merely out of ceremony depart, and the bridegroom and bride are left alone with three or four of the nearest and oldest relations of either side; those of the bridegroom being men, those of the bride, women.

Presently, the bride, attended by these few friends, having withdrawn herself for the purpose, appears at one of the doors of the house, and is led to the bridegroom, who stands ready to receive her. Having now taken their station on a mat placed in the centre of the room, they lay hold of the extremities of a wand about four feet long, by which they continue separated, whilst the old men pronounce some short harangues suitable to the occasion.

The married couple after this make a public declaration of the love and regard they entertain for each other, and still holding the rod between them, dance and sing. When they have finished this part of the ceremony, they break the rod into as many pieces as there are witnesses present, who each take a piece and preserve it with great care.

The bride is then re-conducted out of the door at which she entered, where her young companions wait to attend her to her father's house; there the bridegroom is obliged to seek her and the marriage is consummated. Very often the wife remains at her father's house till she has a child, when she packs up her apparel, which is all the fortune she is generally possessed of, and accompanies her husband to his habitation.

When from any dislike a separation takes place, for they are seldom known to quarrel, they generally give their friends a few days notice of their intentions, and sometimes offer reasons to justify their conduct. The witnesses who were present at the marriage meet on the day requested at the house of the couple that are about to separate, and bringing with them the pieces of rod which they had received at their nuptials, throw them into the fire in the presence of all the parties.

This is the whole of the ceremony required, and the separation is carried on without any murmurings or ill-will between the couple or their relations; and after a few months they are at liberty to marry again.

When a marriage is thus dissolved, the children which have been produced from it, are equally divided between them; and as children are esteemed a treasure by the Indians, if the number happens to be odd, the woman is allowed to take the better half.

Though this custom seems to encourage fickleness and frequent separations, yet there are many of the Indians who have but one wife, and enjoy with her a state of connubial happiness not to be exceeded in more refined societies. There are also not a few instances of women preserving an inviolable attachment to their husbands, except in the cases before-mentioned, which are not considered as either a violation of their chastity or fidelity.

Although I have said that the Indian nations differ very little from each other in their marriage ceremonies, there are some exceptions. The Naudowessies have a singular method of celebrating their marriages which seems to bear no resemblance to those made use of by any other nation I passed through. When one of their young men has fixed on a young woman he approves of, he discovers his passion to her parents who give him an invitation to come and live with them in their tent.

He accordingly accepts the offer, and by so doing engages to reside in it for a whole year in the character of a menial servant. During this time he hunts and brings all the game he kills to the family, by which means the father has an opportunity of seeing whether he is able to provide for the support of his daughter and the children that might be the consequence of their union. This however is only done whilst they are young men, and for their first wife, and not repeated like Jacob's servitudes.

When this period is expired, the marriage is solemnized after the custom of the country, in the following manner: Three or four of the oldest male relations of the bridegroom, and as many of the bride's, accompany the young couple from their respective tents to an open part in the centre of the camp.

The chiefs and warriors being here assembled to receive them, a party of the latter are drawn up in two ranks on each side of the bride and bridegroom immediately on their arrival. The principal chief then acquaints the whole assembly with the design of their meeting and tells them that the couple before them, mentioning at the same time their names, are come to avow publicly their intentions of living together as man and wife. He then asks the two young people alternately, whether they desire that the union might take place. Having declared with an audible voice that they do so, the warriors fix their arrows and discharge them over the heads of the married pair; this done, the chief pronounces them man and wife.

The bridegroom then turns round and, bending his body, takes his wife on his back, in which manner he carries her amidst the acclamations of the spectators to his tent. This ceremony is succeeded by the most plentiful feast the new married man can afford, and songs and dances, according to the usual custom, conclude the festival.

Divorces happen so seldom among the Naudowessies that I had not an opportunity of learning how they are accomplished.

Adultery is esteemed by them a heinous crime and punished with the greatest rigour. The husband in these cases bites off the wife's nose and a separation instantly ensues. I saw an instance wherein this mode of punishment was inflicted whilst I remained among them. The children, when this happens, are distributed according the usual custom observed by other nations, that is, they are equally divided.

Among the Indian as well as European nations, there are many that devote themselves to pleasure and, notwithstanding the accounts given by some modern writers of the frigidity of an Indian constitution, become the zealous votaries of Venus. The young warriors that are thus disposed seldom want opportunities for gratifying their passion; and as the mode usually followed on these occasion is rather singular, I shall describe it.

When one of these young debauchees imagines from the behaviour of the person he has chosen for his mistress, that he shall not meet with any great obstruction to his suit from her, he pursues the following plan.

It has been already observed that the Indians acknowledge no superiority, nor have they any ideas of subordination, except in the necessary regulations of their war or hunting parties; they consequently live nearly in a state of equality pursuant to the first principles of nature. The lover therefore is not apprehensive of any check or control in the accomplishment of his purposes if he can find a convenient opportunity for completing them.

As the Indians are also under no apprehension of robbers or secret enemies, they leave the doors of their tents or huts unfastened during the night, as well as in the day. Two or three hours after sunset, the slaves or old people cover over the fire, that is generally burning in the midst of their apartment, with ashes and retire to their repose.

Whilst darkness thus prevails, and all is quiet, one of these sons of pleasure, wrapped up closely in his blanket to prevent his being known, will sometimes enter the apartment of his intended mistress. Having first lighted at the smothered fire a small splinter of wood, which answers the purpose of a match, he approaches the place where she reposes and, gently pulling away the covering from her head, jogs her till she awakes. If she then rises up and blows out the light, he needs no further confirmation that his company is not disagreeable; but if, after he has discovered himself, she hides her head and takes no notice of him, he might rest assured that any further solicitations will prove vain and that it is necessary immediately for him to retire.

During his stay he conceals the light as much as possible in the hollow of his hands, and as the tents or rooms of the Indians are usually large and capacious, he escapes without detection. It is said that the young women who admit their lovers on these occasions take great care, by an immediate application to herbs, with the potent efficacy of which they are well acquainted, to prevent the effects of these illicit amours from becoming visible; for should the natural consequences ensue, they must for ever remain unmarried.

The children of the Indians are always distinguished by the name of the mother; and if a woman marries several husbands and has issue by each of them, they are all called after her. The reason they give for this is that as their offspring are indebted to the father for their souls, the invisible part of their essence, and to the mother for their corporeal and apparent part, it is more rational that they should be distinguished by the name of the latter, from whom they indubitably derive their being, than by that of the father, to which a doubt might sometimes arise whether they are justly intitled.

There are some ceremonies made use of by the Indians at the imposition of the name, and it is considered by them as a matter of great importance; but what these are I could never learn, through the secrecy observed on the occasion. I only know that it is usually given when the children have passed the state of infancy.

Nothing can exceed the tenderness shown by them to their offspring; and a person cannot recommend himself to their favour by any method more certain than by paying some attention to the younger branches of their families. I can impute, in some measure, to the presents I made to the children of the chiefs of the Naudowessies the hospitable reception I met with when among them.

Some difficulty attends an explanation of the manner in which the Indians distinguish themselves from each other. Besides the name of the animal by which every nation and tribe is denominated, there are others that are personal and which the children receive from their mother.

The chiefs are also distinguished by a name that has either some reference to their abilities or to the hieroglyphicks of their families, and these are acquired after they arrive at the age of manhood. Such as have signalized themselves either in their war or hunting parties, or are possessed of some eminent qualification, receive a name that serves to perpetuate the fame of these actions or to make their abilities conspicuous.

Thus the great warrior of the Naudowessies was named Ottahtongoomlishcah*, that is, the Great Father of Snakes, ottah being in English father, tongoom great, and lishcah a snake. Another chief was called Honahpawjatin*, which means a swift runner over the mountains. And when they adopted me a chief among them, they named me Shebaygo, which signifies a writer, or a person that is curious in making hieropglyphicks, as they saw me often writing.

* Presumably these are the chiefs mentioned on page 48, though the spelling of their names is slightly different.

CHAPTER XII

Of Their Religion

I T IS VERY difficult to attain a perfect knowledge of the religious principles of the Indians. Their ceremonies and doctrines have been so often ridiculed by the Europeans that they endeavour to conceal them; and if, after the greatest intimacy, you desire any of them to explain to you their system of religion, to prevent your ridicule they intermix with it many of the tenets they have received from the French missionaries, so that it is at last rendered an unintelligible jargon, and not to be depended upon.

Such as I could discover among the Naudowessies, for they also were very reserved in this point, I shall give my readers, without paying any attention to the accounts of others. As the religion of that people from their situation appears to be totally unadulterated with the superstitions of the church of Rome, we shall be able to gain from their religious customs a more perfect idea of the original tenets and ceremonies of the Indians in general than from those of any nations that approach nearer to the settlements.

It is certain they acknowledge one Supreme Being or Giver of

Life, who presides over all things. The Chipeways call this being Manitou or Kitchi-Manitou; the Naudowessies, Wakon or Tongo-Wakon, that is, the Great Spirit; and they look up to him as the source of good from whom no evil can proceed. They also believe in a bad spirit to whom they ascribe great power, and suppose that through his means all the evils which befall mankind are inflicted. To him therefore do they pray in their distresses, begging that he would either avert their troubles, or moderate them when they are no longer avoidable.

They say that the Great Spirit, who is infinitely good, neither wishes or is able to do any mischief to mankind; but on the contrary, that he showers down on them all the blessings they deserve; whereas the evil spirit is continually employed in contriving how he may punish the human race; and to do which he is not only possessed of the will, but of the power.

They hold also that there are good spirits of a lesser degree who have their particular departments, in which they are constantly contributing to the happiness of mortals. These they suppose to preside over all the extraordinary productions of nature, such as those lakes, rivers, or mountains that are of an uncommon magnitude; and likewise the beasts, birds, fishes, and even vegetables or stones that exceed the rest of their species in size or singularity. To all of these they pay some kind of adoration. Thus when they arrive on the borders of Lake Superior, on the banks of the Mississippi, or any other great body of water, they present to the Spirit who resides there some kinds of offering, as the prince of the Winnebagoes did when he attended me to the Falls of St. Anthony.

But at the same time I fancy that the ideas they annex to the word spirit are very different from the conceptions more enlightened nations entertain of it. They appear to fashion themselves corporeal representations of their gods, and believe them to be of a human form, though of a nature more excellent than man.

Of the same kind are the sentiments relative to a futurity. They doubt not but they shall exist in some future state; they however fancy that their employments there will be similar to those they are engaged in here, without the labour and difficulty annexed to them in the period of their existence.

They consequently expect to be translated to a delightful country where they shall always have a clear unclouded sky and enjoy a perpetual spring; where the forests will abound with game, and the lakes with fish, which might be taken without requiring a painful exertion of skill or a laborious pursuit; in short, that they shall live for ever in regions of plenty and enjoy every gratification they delight in here, in a greater degree.

To intellectual pleasures they are strangers; nor are these included in their scheme of happiness. But they expect that even these animal pleasures will be proportioned and distributed according to their merit; the skilful hunter, the bold and successful warrior, will be entitled to a greater share than those who through indolence or want of skill cannot boast of any superiority over the common herd.

The priests of the Indians are at the same time their physicians and their conjurors; whilst they heal their wounds or cure their diseases, they interpret their dreams, give them protective charms, and satisfy that desire which is so prevalent among them of searching into futurity.

How well they execute the latter part of their professional engagements, and the methods they make use of on some of these occasions, I have already shewn in the exertions of the priest of the Killistinoes, who was fortunate enough to succeed in his extraordinary attempt near Lake Superior. They frequently are successful likewise in administering the salubrious herbs they have acquired a knowledge of; but that the ceremonies they make use of during the administration of them contributes to their success, I shall not take upon me to assert.

When any of the people are ill, the person who is invested with this triple character of doctor, priest, and magician, sits by the patient day and night, rattling in his ears a goad-shell filled with dry beans, called a chichicoue, and making a disagreeable noise that cannot be well described.

This uncouth harmony one would imagine should disturb the sick person and prevent the good effects of the doctor's prescription; but on the contrary they believe that the method made use of contributes to his recovery by diverting from his malignant purposes the evil spirit who has inflicted the disorder; or at least that it will take off his attention, so that he shall not increase the malady. This they are credulous enough to imagine he is constantly on the watch to do, and would carry his inveteracy to a fatal length if they did not thus charm him.

I could not discover that they make use of any other religious ceremonies than those I have described; indeed, on the appearance of the new moon they dance and sing. But it is not evident that they pay that planet any adoration; they only seem to rejoice at the return of a luminary that makes the night cheerful and which serves to light them on their way when they travel during the absence of the sun.

Notwithstanding Mr. Adair has asserted that the nations among whom he resided, observe with very little variation all the rites appointed by the Mosaic Law, I own I could never discover among those tribes that lie but a few degrees to the northwest the least traces of the Jewish religion, except it be admitted that one particular female custom* and their division into tribes, carry with them proofs sufficient to establish this assertion.

The Jesuits and French missionaries have also pretended that the Indians had, when they first travelled into America, some notions, though these were dark and confused, of the Christian institution; that they have been greatly agitated at the sight of a cross, and given proofs, by the impressions made on them, that they were not entirely unacquainted with the sacred mysteries of Christianity. I need not say that these are too glaring absurdities to be credited and could only receive their existence from the zeal of those fathers who endeavoured at once to give the public a better opinion of the success of their missions, and to add support to the cause they were engaged in.

The Indians appear to be in their religious principles rude and uninstructed. The doctrines they hold are few and simple, and such as have been generally impressed on the human mind by some means or

* Presumably a reference to conduct during menstruation (see Chapter III).

other in the most ignorant ages. They however have not deviated, as many other uncivilized nations and too many civilized ones have done, into idolatrous modes of worship. They venerate indeed and make offerings to the wonderful parts of creation, as I have before observed; but whether these rites are performed on account of the impressions such extraordinary appearances make on them, or whether they consider them as the peculiar charge or the usual places of residence of the invisible spirits they acknowledged, I cannot positively determine.

The human mind in its uncultivated state is apt to ascribe the extraordinary occurrences of nature, such as earthquakes, thunder or hurricanes, to the interposition of unseen being; the troubles and disasters also that are annexed to a savage life, the apprehensions attendant on a precarious susbsistence, and those numberless inconveniences which man in his improvident state has found means to remedy, are supposed to proceed from the interposition of evil spirits. The savage consequently lives in continual apprehensions of their unkind attacks, and to avert them has recourse to charms, to the fantastic ceremonies of his priest, or the powerful influence of his Manitous. Fear has of course a greater share in his devotions than gratitude, and he pays more attention to deprecating the wrath of the evil than to securing the favour of the good beings.

The Indians, however, entertain these absurdities in common with those of every part of the globe who have not been illumined by that religion which only can disperse the clouds of superstition and ignorance, and they are as free from error as a people can be that has not been favoured with its instructive doctrines.

CHAPTER XIII

Of Their Diseases

THE INDIANS in general are healthy and subject but to few diseases, many of those that afflict civilized nations and are the immediate consequences of luxury or sloth being not known among them. However the hardships and fatigues which they endure in hunting or war, the inclemency of the seasons to which they are continually exposed, but above all the extremes of hunger and that voraciousness their long excursions consequently subject them to, cannot fail of impairing the constitution and bringing on disorders.

Pains and weaknesses in the stomach and breast are sometimes the result of their long fasting and consumptions of the excessive fatigue and violent exercises they expose themselves to from their infancy, before they have strength sufficient to support them. But the disorder to which they are most subject is the pleurisy, for the removal of which they apply their grand remedy and preservative against the generality of their complaints, sweating.

The manner in which they construct their stoves for this purpose is as follows: They fix several small poles in the ground, the tops of which they twist together so as to form a rotunda. This frame they cover with skins or blankets and they lay them on with so much nicety that the air is kept from entering through any crevice, a small space being only left just sufficient to creep in at, which is immediately after closed. In the middle of this confined building they place red hot stones on which they pour water till a steam arises that produces a great degree of heat.

This causes an instantaneous perspiration which they increase as they please. Having continued in it for some time, they immediately hasten to the nearest stream and plunge into the water and, after bathing therein for about half a minute, they put on their cloaths, sit down and smoke with great composure, thoroughly persuaded that the remedy will prove efficacious. They often make use of this sudoriferous method to refresh themselves or to prepare their minds for the management of any business that requires uncommon deliberations and sagacity.

They are likewise afflicted with the dropsy and paralytic complaints which, however, are but very seldom known among them. As a remedy for these as well as for fevers, they make use of lotions and decoctions composed of herbs which the physicians know perfectly well how to compound and apply. But they never trust to medicines alone; they always have recourse likewise to some superstitious ceremonies, without which their patients would not think the physical preparations sufficiently powerful.

With equal judgment they make use of simples for the cure of wounds, fractures, or bruises, and are able to heal by these, without incision, splinters, iron, or any sort of matter by which the wound is caused. In cures of this kind, they are extremely dextrous and complete them in much less time than might be expected from their mode of proceeding.

With the skin of a snake, which those reptiles annually shed, they will also extract splinters. It is amazing to see the sudden efficacy of this application, notwithstanding there does not appear to be the least moisture remaining in it.

It has long been a subject of dispute, on what continent the venereal disease first received its destructive power. This dreadful malady is supposed to have originated in America, but the literary contest still remains undecided. To give some elucidation to it I shall remark, that as I could not discover the least traces among the Naudowessies with whom I resided so long, and was also informed that it was yet unknown among the more western nations, I think I may venture to pronounce that it had not its origin in North America. Those nations that have any communication with the Europeans or the southern tribes are greatly afflicted with it; but they have all of them acquired a knowledge of such certain and expeditious remedies that the communication is not attended with any dangerous consequences.

Soon after I set out on my travels, one of the traders whom I accompanied, complained of a violent gonorrhoea, with all its alarming symptoms. This increased to such a degree that by the time we had reached the town of the Winnebagoes, he was unable to travel. Having made his complaint known to one of the chiefs of that tribe, he told him not to be uneasy for he would engage that by following his advice, he should be able in a few days to pursue his journey and in a little longer time be entirely free from his disorder.

The chief had no sooner said this than he prepared for him a decoction of the bark of the roots of the prickly Ash, a tree scarcely known in England but which grows in great plenty throughout North America; by the use of which in a few days he was greatly recovered and, having received directions how to prepare it, in a fortnight after his departure from this place perceived that he was radically cured.

If from excessive exercise or the extremes of heat or cold, they are affected with pains in their limbs or joints, they scarify the parts affected. Those nations who have no commerce with Europeans do this with a sharp flint and it is surprizing to see to how fine a point they have the dexterity to bring them; a lancet can scarcely exceed in sharpness the instruments they make of this unmalleable substance.

They never can be convinced a person is ill whilst he has an appetite. But when he rejects all kind of nourishment, they consider the disease as dangerous and pay great attention to it; and during the continuance of the disorder, the physician refuses his patient no sort of food that he is desirous of.

Their doctors are only supposed to be skilled in the physical treatment of diseases, but the common people believe that by the ceremony of the chichicoue usually made use of, as before described, they are able to gain intelligence from the spirits of the cause of the complaints with which they are afflicted, and are thereby the better enabled to find remedies for them. They discover something supernatural in all their diseases and the physic administered must invariably be aided by these superstitions.

Sometimes a sick person fancies that the disorder arises from witchcraft. In this case the physician or juggler is consulted who, after the usual preparations, gives his opinion on the state of the disease and frequently finds some means for his cure. But notwithstanding the Indian physicians always annex these superstitious ceremonies to their prescriptions, it is very certain, as I have already observed, that they exercise their art by principles which are founded on the knowledge of simples and on experience which they acquire by an indefatigable attention to their operations.

The following story, which I received from a person of undoubted credit, proves that the Indians are not only able to reason with great acuteness on the causes and symptoms of many of the disorders which are attendant on human nature, but to apply with equal judgment proper remedies.

In Penobscot, a settlement in the province of Main, in the northeast parts of New England, the wife of a soldier was taken in labour and, notwithstanding every necessary assistance was given her, could not be delivered. In this situation she remained for two or three days, the persons around her expecting that the next pang would put an end to her existence.

An Indian woman, who accidentally passed by, heard the groans of the unhappy sufferer and enquired from whence they proceeded. Being made acquainted with the desperate circumstances attending the case, she told the informant that if she might be permitted to see the person, she did not doubt but that she could be of great service to her.

The surgeon that had attended and the midwife who was then present having given up every hope of preserving their patient, the Indian woman was allowed to make use of any methods she thought proper. She accordingly took a handkerchief and bound it tight over the nose and mouth of the woman. This immediately brought on a suffocation and from the struggles that consequently ensued she was in a few seconds delivered. The moment this was achieved, and time enough to prevent any fatal effect, the handkerchief was taken off. The long suffering patient, thus happily relieved from her pains, soon after perfectly recovered to the astonishment of all those who had been witness to her desperate situation.

The reason given by the Indian for this hazardous method of proceeding was that desperate disorders require desperate remedies; that as she observed the exertions of nature were not sufficiently forcible to effect the desired consequence, she thought it necessary to augment their force, which could only be done by some mode that was violent in the extreme.

CHAPTER XIV

Of the Manner in Which They Treat Their Dead

AN INDIAN meets death when it approaches him in his hut with the same resolution he has often faced him in the field. His indifference relative to this important article, which is the source of so many apprehensions to almost every other nation, is truly admirable. When his fate is pronounced by the physician, and it remains no longer uncertain, he harangues those about him with the greatest composure.

If he is a chief and has a family, he makes a kind of funeral oration which he concludes by giving to his children such advice for the regulation of their conduct as he thinks necessary. He then takes leave of his friends, and issues out orders for the preparation of a feast, which is designed to regale those of his tribe that come to pronounce his eulogium.

After the breath is departed, the body is dressed in the same attire it usually wore whilst living, his face is painted, and he is seated in an erect posture on a mat or skin placed in the middle of the hut, with his weapons by his side. His relations being seated round, each harangues in turn the deceased; and if he has been a great warrior, recounts his heroic actions nearly to the following purport, which in the Indian language is extremely poetical and pleasing:

"You still sit among us, Brother, your person retains its usual resemblance, and continues similar to ours, without any visible deficiency, except that it has lost the power of action. But whither is that breath flown which a few hours ago sent up smoke to the Great Spirit? Why are those lips silent that lately delivered to us expressive and pleasing language? Why are those feet motionless that a short time ago were fleeter than the deer on yonder mountains? Why useless hang those arms that could climb the tallest tree or draw the toughest bow? Alas! every part of that frame which we lately beheld with admiration and wonder is now become as inanimate as it was three hundred winters ago. We will not, however, bemoan thee as if thou wast for ever lost to us, or that thy name would be buried in oblivion; thy soul yet lives in the great Country of Spirits with those of thy nation that are gone before thee and, though we are left behind to perpetuate thy fame, we shall one day join thee. Actuated by the respect we bore thee whilst living, we now come to tender thee the last act of kindness it is in our power to bestow: that thy body might not lie neglected on the plain and become a prey to the beasts of the field or the fowls of the air, we will take care to lay it with those of thy predecessors who are gone before thee, hoping at the same time that thy spirit will feed with their spirits, and be ready to receive ours when we also shall arrive at the great Country of Souls."

In short speeches somewhat similar to this does every chief speak the praise of his departed friend. When they have so done, if they happen to be at a great distance from the place of interment appropriated to their tribe, and the person dies during the winter season, they wrap the body in skins and lay it on a high stage built for this purpose, or on the branches of a large tree, till the spring arrives. They then carry it, together with all those belonging to the same nation, to the general burial-place where it is interred with some other ceremonies that I could not discover.

When the Naudowessies brought their dead for interment to the great cave, I attempted to get an insight into the remaining burial rites; but whether it was on account of the stench which arose from so many bodies, the weather being then hot, or whether they chose to keep this part of their customs secret from me, I could not discover. I found, however, that they considered my curiosity as ill-timed and therefore I withdrew.

After the interment, the band to which the person belongs take care to fix near the place such hieroglyphicks as shall show to future ages his merit and accomplishments. If any of these people die in the summer at a distance from the burying-ground, and they find it impossible to remove the body before it putrifies, they burn the flesh from the bones, and preserving the latter, bury them in the manner described.

As the Indians believe that the souls of the deceased employ themselves in the same manner in the country of spirits as they did on earth, that they acquire their food by hunting, and have there also enemies to contend with, they take care that they do not enter those regions defenceless and unprovided. They consequently bury with them their bows, their arrows, and all the other weapons used either in hunting or war. As they doubt not but they will likewise have occasion both for the necessaries of life and those things they esteem as ornaments, they usually deposit in their tombs such skins or stuff as they commonly made their garments of, domestic utensils, and paint for ornamenting their persons.

The near relations of the deceased lament his loss with an appearance of great sorrow and anguish; they weep and howl and make use of many contortions as they sit in the hut or tent around the body, when the intervals between the praises of the chiefs will permit.

One formality in mourning for the dead among the Naudowessies is very different from any mode I observed in the other nations through which I passed. The men, to show how great their sorrow is, pierce the flesh of their arms above the elbows with arrows, the scars of which I could perceive on those of every rank, in a greater or less degree; and the women cut and gash their legs with sharp broken flints till the blood flows very plentifully.

Whilst I remained among them, a couple whose tent was adjacent to mine lost a son about four years of age. The parents were so much affected at the death of their favourite child that they pursued the usual testimonies of grief with such uncommon rigour as, through the weight of sorrow and loss of blood, to occasion the death of the father. The woman, who had hitherto been inconsolable, no sooner saw her husband expire than she dried up her tears and appeared cheerful and resigned.

As I knew not how to account for so extraordinary a transition, I took an opportunity to ask her the reason of it, telling her at the same time that I should have imagined the loss of her husband would rather have occasioned an increase of grief than such a sudden dimunition of it.

She informed me that as the child was so young when it died and unable to support itself in the country of spirits, both she and her husband had been apprehensive that its situation would be far from happy; but no sooner did she behold its father depart for the same place, who not only loved the child with the tenderest affection but was a good hunter and would be able to provide plentifully for its support, than she ceased to mourn. She added, that she now saw no reason to continue her tears, as the child on whom she doted was happy under the care and protection of a fond father, and she had only one wish that remained ungratified, which was that of being herself with them.

Expressions so replete with unaffected tenderness, and sentiments that would have done honour to a Roman matron, made an impression on my mind greatly in favour of the people to whom she belonged and tended not a little to counteract the prejudices I had hitherto entertained, in common with every other traveller, of Indian insensibility and want of parental tenderness.

Her subsequent conduct confirmed the favourable opinion I had just imbibed and convinced me that, notwithstanding this apparent suspension of her grief, some particles of that reluctance to be separated from a beloved relation, which is implanted either by nature or custom in every human heart, still lurked in hers. I observed that she went almost every evening to the foot of the tree, on a branch of which the bodies of her husband and child were laid, and after cutting a lock of her hair and throwing it on the ground, in a plaintive melancholy song bemoaned its fate. A recapitulation of the actions he might have performed, had his life been spared, appeared to be her favourite theme; and whilst she foretold the fame that would have attended an imitation of his father's virtues, her grief seemed to be suspended:

"If thou hadst continued with us, my dear Son," would she cry, "how well would the bow have become thy hand, and how fatal would thy arrows have proved to the enemies of our bands. Thou wouldst often have drank their blood and eaten their flesh, and numerous slaves would have rewarded thy toils. With a nervous arm wouldst thou have seized the wounded buffalo or have combated the fury of the enraged bear. Thou wouldst have overtaken the flying elk, and have kept pace on the mountain's brow with the fleetest deer. What feats mightest thou not have performed hadst thou staid among us till age had given thee strength, and thy father had instructed thee in every Indian accomplishment!" In terms like these did this untutored savage bewail the loss of her son, and frequently would she pass the greatest part of the night in the affectionate employ.

The Indians in general are very strict in the observance of their laws relative to mourning for their dead. In some nations they cut off their hair, blacken their faces, and sit in an erect posture, with their heads closely covered, and depriving themselves of every pleasure. This severity is continued for several months, and with some relaxations the appearance is sometimes kept up for several years. I was told that when the Naudowessies recollected any incidents of the lives of their deceased relations, even after an interval of ten years, they would howl so as to be heard at a great distance. They would sometimes continue this proof of respect and affection for several hours; and if it happened that the thought occurred and the noise was begun towards the evening, those of their tribe who were at hand would join with them.

CHAPTER XV

A Concise Character
of the Indians

THE CHARACTER of the Indians, like that of other uncivilized nations, is composed of a mixture of ferocity and gen-
tleness. They are at once guided by passions and appetites, which they
hold in common with the fiercest beasts that inhabit their woods, and
are possessed of virtues which do honour to human nature.

In the following estimate I shall endeavour to forget on the one
hand the prejudices of Europeans, who usually annex to the word
Indian epithets that are disgraceful to human nature, and who view
them in no other light than as savages and cannibals; whilst with equal
care I avoid any partiality towards them, as some must naturally arise
from the favourable reception I met with during my stay among
them.

At the same time I shall confine my remarks to the nations inhabiting only the western regions, such as the Naudowessies, the Ottagaumies, the Chipeways, the Winnebagoes, and the Saukies; for as
throughout that diversity of climates the extensive continent of America is composed of there are people of different dispositions and

various characters, it would be incompatible with my present under-taking to treat all these and to give a general view of them as a conjunctive body.

That the Indians are of a cruel, revengeful, inexorable disposition, that they will watch whole days unmindful of the calls of nature, and make their way through pathless and almost unbounded woods, sub-sisting only on the scanty produce of them, to pursue and revenge themselves of an enemy; that they hear unmoved the piercing cries of such as unhappily fall into their hands, and receive a diabolical pleasure from the tortures they inflict on their prisoners, I readily grant. But let us look on the reverse of this terrifying picture and we shall find them temperate both in their diet and potations (it must be remembered, that I speak of those tribes who have little communica-tion with Europeans) that they withstand, with unexampled patience, the attacks of hunger or the inclemency of the seasons, and esteem the gratification of their appetites but as a secondary consideration.

We shall likewise see them sociable and humane to those they consider as their friends and even to their adopted enemies, and ready to partake with them of the last morsel, or to risk their lives in their defence.

In contradiction to the reports of many other travellers, all of which have been tinctured with prejudice, I can assert, that notwith-standing the apparent indifference with which an Indian meets his wife and children after a long absence, an indifference proceeding rather from custom than insensibility, he is not unmindful of the claims either of connubial or parental tenderness; the little story I have introduced in the preceding chapter of the Naudowessie woman lamenting her child, and the immature death of the father, will elucidate this point and enforce the assertion much better than the most studied arguments I can make use of.

Accustomed from their youth to innumerable hardships, they soon become superior to a sense of danger, or the dread of death; and their fortitude, implanted by nature and nurtured by example, by precept, and accident, never experiences a moment's allay.

Though slothful and inactive whilst their store of provision remains unexhausted and their foes are at a distance, they are indefatig-able and persevering in pursuit of their game or in circumventing their enemies.

If they are artful and designing and ready to take every advantage, if they are cool and deliberate in their councils, and cautious in the extreme either of discovering their sentiments or of revealing a se-cret, they might at the same time boast of possessing qualifications of a more animated nature, of the sagacity of a hound, the penetrating sight of a lynx, the cunning of the fox, the agility of a bounding roe, and the unconquerable fierceness of the tyger.

In their public characters, as forming part of a community, they possess an attachment for that band to which they belong unknown to the inhabitants of any other country. They combine, as if they were actuated only by one soul, against the enemies of their nation and banish from their minds every consideration opposed to this.

They consult without unnecessary opposition, or without giving way to the excitements of envy or ambition, on the measures necessary to be pursued for the destruction of those who have drawn on them-selves their displeasure. No selfish views ever influence their advice or obstruct their consultations. Nor is it in the power of bribes or threats to diminish the love they bear their country.

The honour of their tribe and the welfare of their nation is the first and most predominant emotion of their hearts; and from hence pro-ceed in a great measure all their virtues and their vices. Actuated by this, they brave every danger, endure the most exquisite torments, and expire triumphing in their fortitude, not as a personal qualifica-tion, but as a national characteristic.

From thence also flow that insatiable revenge towards those with whom they are at war and all the consequent horrors that disgrace their name. Their uncultivated mind, being incapable of judging of the propriety of an action in opposition to their passions, which are totally insensible to the controls of reason or humanity, they know not how to keep their fury within any bounds. Consequently that courage and resolution, which would otherwise do them honour, degenerates into a savage ferocity.

But this short dissertation must suffice; the limits of my work will not permit me to treat the subject more copiously or to pursue it with a logical regularity. The observations already made for my readers on the preceding pages will, I trust, render it unnecessary; as by them they will be enabled to form a tolerably just idea of the people I have been describing. Experience teaches that anecdotes and relations of particular events, however trifling they might appear, enable us to form a truer judgment of the manners and customs of a people, and are much more declaratory of their real state than the most studied and elaborate disquisition without these aids.

CHAPTER XVI

Of Their Hieroglyphicks

ALTHOUGH THE Indians cannot communicate their ideas by writing, yet they form certain hieroglyphicks which, in some measure, serve to perpetuate any extraordinary transaction or uncommon event. Thus when they are on their excursions, and either intend to proceed or have been on any remarkable enterprize, they peel the bark from the trees which lie in their way, to give intelligence to those parties that happen to be at a distance of the path they must pursue to overtake them.

The following instance will convey a more perfect idea of the methods they make use of on this occasion than any expressions I can frame.

When I left the Mississippi, and proceeded up the Chipeway River on my way to Lake Superior, as related in my Journal, my guide, who was a chief of the Chipeways that dwell on the Ottowaw Lake near the heads of the river we had just entered, fearing that some parties of Naudowessies, with whom his nation are perpetually at war might accidentally fall in with us and, before they were apprized of my being in company, do us some mischief, he took the following steps.

He peeled the bark from a large tree near the entrance of a river and with wood-coal mixed with bear's-grease, their usual substitute for ink, made in an uncouth but expressive manner the figure of the town of the Ottagaumies. He then formed to the left a man dressed in skins, by which he intended to represent a Naudowessie, with a line drawn from his mouth to that of a deer, the symbol of the Chipeways. After this he depictured still farther to the left a canoe as proceeding up the river, in which he placed a man sitting with a hat on; this figure was designed to represent an Englishman, or myself, and my Frenchman was drawn with a handkerchief tied round his head and rowing the canoe. To these he added several other significant emblems, among which the Pipe of Peace appeared painted on the prow of the canoe.

The meaning he intended to convey to the Naudowessies, and which I doubt not appeared perfectly intelligible to them, was that one of the Chipeway chiefs had received a speech from some Naudowessie chiefs at the town of the Ottagaumies, desiring him to conduct the Englishman, who had lately been among them, up the Chipeway River; and that they thereby required that the Chipeway, notwithstanding he was an avowed enemy, should not be molested by them on his passage, as he had the care of a person whom they esteemed as one of their nation.

Some authors have pretended that the Indians have armorial bearings, which they blazon with great exactness, and which distinguish one nation from another. But I never could observe any other arms among them than the symbols already described.

CHAPTER XVII

Of the Beasts Which Are Found in the Interior Parts of North America

O F THESE, I shall, in the first place give a catalogue and afterwards a description of such only as are either peculiar to this country, or which differ in some material point from those that are to be met with in other realms.

OF THE BEASTS

The Tyger, the Bear, Wolves, Foxes, Dogs, the Cat of the Mountain, the Wild Cat, the Buffalo, the Deer, the Elk, the Moose, the Carribbou, the Carcajou, the Skunk, the Porcupine, the Hedge-hog, the Wood-chuck, the Raccoon, the Martin, the Fisher, the Musk-quaw, Squirrels, Hares, Rabbits, the Mole, the Weezel, the Mouse, the Dormouse, the Beaver, the Otter, the Mink, and Bats.

The TYGER. The Tyger of America resembles in shape those of Africa and Asia, but is considerably smaller. Nor does it appear to be so fierce and ravenous as they are. The colour of it is a darkish fallow and it is entirely free from spots. I saw one on an island in the

Chipeway River, of which I had a very good view as it was at no great distance from me. It sat up on its hinder parts like a dog and did not seem either to be apprehensive of our approach or to discover any ravenous inclinations. It is however very seldom to be met with in this part of the world.

The BEAR. Bears are very numerous on this continent, but more particularly so in the northern parts of it, and contribute to furnish both food and beds for almost every Indian nation. Those of America differ in many respects from those either in Greenland or Russia, they being not only somewhat smaller, but timorous and inoffensive, unless they are pinched by hunger or smarting from a wound. The sight of a man terrifies them and a dog will put several to flight. They are extremely fond of grapes, and will climb to the top of the highest trees in quest of them. This kind of food renders their flesh excessively rich and finely flavoured and it is consequently preferred by the Indians and traders to that of any other animal. The fat is very white, and besides being sweet and wholesome, is possessed of one valuable quality, which is, that it never cloys. The inhabitants of these parts constantly anoint themselves with it, and to its efficacy they in a great measure owe their agility.

The WOLF. The wolves of North America are much less than those which are met with in other parts of the world. They have, however, in common with the rest of their species, a wildness in their looks and a fierceness in their eyes; notwithstanding which they are far from being so ravenous as the European wolves, nor will they ever attack a man, except they have accidentally fed on the flesh of those slain in battle. When they herd together, as they often do in winter, they make a hideous and terrible noise. In these parts there are two kinds; one of which is of a fallow colour, the other of a dun, inclining to black.

The FOX. There are two sorts of foxes in North America, which differ only in their colour, one being of a reddish brown, the other of a grey. Those of the latter kind that are found near the river Mississippi are extremely beautiful, their hair being of a fine silver grey.

DOGS. The dogs employed by the Indians in hunting appear to be all of the same species. They carry their ears erect and greatly resemble a wolf about the head. They are exceedingly useful to them in their hunting excursions and will attack the fiercest of the game they are in pursuit of. They are also remarkable for their fidelity to their masters but, being ill fed by them, are very troublesome in their huts or tents.

The CAT OF THE MOUNTAIN. This creature is in shape like a cat, only much larger. The hair or fur resembles also the skin of that domestic animal. The colour however differs, for the former is of a reddish or orange cast but grows lighter near the belly. The whole skin is beautified with black spots of different figures, of which those on the back are long and those on the lower parts round. On the ears there are black stripes. This creature is nearly as fierce as a leopard, but will seldom attack a man.

The BUFFALO. This beast, of which there are amazing numbers in these parts, is larger than an ox, has short black horns, with a large beard under his chin, and his head is so full of hair that it falls over his eyes and gives him a frightful look. There is a hunch on his back which begins at the haunches and, increasing gradually to the shoulders, reaches on to the neck. Both this excrescence and its whole body are covered with long hair, or rather wool, of a dun or mouse colour which is exceedingly valuable, especially that on the fore part of the body. Its head is larger than a bull's, with a very short neck; the breast is broad, and the body decreases towards the buttocks. These creatures will run away at the sight of a man, and a whole herd will make off when they perceive a single dog. The flesh of the buffalo is excellent food, its hide extremely useful, and the hair very proper for the manufacture of various articles.

The DEER. There is but one species of deer in North America, and these are higher and of a slimmer make than those in Europe. Their shape is nearly the same as the European, their colour of a deep fallow, and their horns very large and branching. This beast is the swiftest on the American plains, and they herd together as they do in other countries.

The ELK greatly exceeds the deer in size, being in bulk equal to a horse. Its body is shaped like that of a deer, only its tail is remarkably short, being not more than three inches long. The colour of its hair, which is grey, and not unlike that of a camel, but of a more reddish cast, is nearly three inches in length, and as coarse as that of a horse. The horns of this creature grow to a prodigious size, extending so wide that two or three persons might fit between them at the same time. They are not forked like those of a deer, but have all their teeth or branches on the outer edge. Nor does the form of those of the elk resemble a deer's; the former being flat, and eight or ten inches broad, whereas the latter are round and considerably narrower. They shed their horns every year in the month of February and by August the new ones are nearly arrived at their full growth. Notwithstanding their size, and the means of defence nature has furnished them with, they are as timorous as a deer.

The MOOSE is nearly about the size of the elk, and the horns of it are almost as enormous as that animal's; the stem of them however are not quite so wide, and they branch on both sides like those of a deer. This creature also sheds them every year. Though its hinder parts are very broad, its tail is not above an inch long. It has feet and legs like a camel; its head is about two feet long, its upper lip much larger than the under, and the nostrils of it are so wide that a man might thrust his hand into them a considerable way.

The CARRIBBOU. This beast is not near so tall as the moose, however it is something like it in shape, only rather more heavy, and inclining to the form of the ass. The horns of it are not flat as those of the elk are, but round like those of the deer; they also meet nearer together at the extremities, and bend more over the face, than either those of the elk or the moose.

The CARCAJOU. This creature, which is of the cat kind, is a terrible enemy to the preceding four species of beasts. He either comes upon them from concealment unperceived, or climbs up into a tree, and taking his station on some of the branches, waits till one of them, driven by an extreme of heat or cold, takes shelter under it;

when he fastens upon his neck and, opening the jugular vein, soon brings his prey to the ground. This he is enabled to do by his long tail, with which he encircles the body of his adversary; and the only means they have to shun their fate, is by flying immediately to the water. By this method, as the carcajou has a great dislike of that element, he is sometimes got rid of before he can effect his purpose.

The SKUNK. This is the most extraordinary animal that the American woods produce. It is rather less than a pole-cat, and of the same species. It is therefore often mistaken for that creature, but is very different from it in many points. Its hair is long and shining, variegated with large black and white spots, the former mostly on the shoulders and rump. Its tail is very bushy, like that of the fox, part black and part white, like its body. It lives chiefly in the woods and hedges. But its extraordinary powers are only shewn when it is pursued. As soon as he finds himself in danger, he ejects, to a great distance from behind, a small stream of water of so subtile a nature and at the same time of so powerful a smell that the air is tainted with it for half a mile in circumference, and his pursuers, whether men or dogs, being almost suffocated with the stench, are obliged to give over the pursuit. It is almost impossible to describe the noisome effects of the liquid with which this creature is supplied by nature for its defence. If a drop of it falls on your cloaths, they are rendered so disagreeable that it is impossible ever after to wear them; or if any of it enters your eyelids, the pain becomes intolerable for a long time, and perhaps at last you lose your sight.

The PORCUPINE. The body of the American porcupine is in bulk about the size of a small dog, but it is both shorter in length and not so high from the ground. It varies very much from those of other countries both in its shape and the length of its quills. The former is like that of a fox, except the head which is not so sharp and long, but resembles more that of a rabbit. Its body is covered with hair of a dark brown, about four inches long, great parts of which are the thickness of a straw, and are termed its quills. These are white, with black points, hollow, and very strong, especially those that grow on the back. The quills serve this creature for offensive and defensive weapons which he darts at his enemies, and if they pierce the flesh in the least degree, they will sink quite into it, and are not to be extracted without incision. The Indians use them for boring their ears and noses to insert their pendants, and also by way of ornament to their stockings, hair, &c. besides which they greatly esteem the flesh.

The WOOD-CHUCK is a ground animal of the fur kind, about the size of a martin, being nearly fifteen inches long; its body however is rounder, and its legs shorter; the fore paws of it are broad and constructed for the purpose of digging holes in the ground, where it burrows like a rabbit. Its fur is of a grey colour on the reddish cast and its flesh tolerable food.

The RACCOON is somewhat less in size than a beaver, and its feet and legs are like those of that creature, but short in proportion to its body which resembles that of a badger. The shape of its head is much like a fox's, only the ears are shorter, more round and naked; and its hair is also similar to that animal's, being thick, long, soft, and black at the ends. On its face there is a broad stripe that runs across it and includes the eyes which are large. Its muzzle is black and the end roundish like those of a dog in number and shape; the tail is long and round, with annular stripes on it like those of a cat; the feet have five long slender toes armed with sharp claws, by which it is enabled to climb up trees like a monkey and to run to the very extremities of the boughs. It makes use of its fore feet in the manner of hands, and feeds itself with them.

The MARTIN is rather larger than a squirrel and somewhat of the same make. Its legs and claws however are considerably shorter. Its ears are short, broad and roundish, and its eyes shine in the night like those of a cat. The whole body is covered with fur of a brownish fallow colour and there are some in the more northern parts which are black. The skins of the latter are of much greater value than the others. The tail is covered with long hair, which makes it appear thicker than it really is. Its flesh is sometimes eaten, but is not in any great esteem.

The MUSQUASH, or MUSK-RAT, is so termed for the exquisite musk which it affords. It appears to be a diminutive of the beaver, being endowed with all the properties of that sagacious animal, and wants nothing but size and strength, being not much bigger than a large rat of the Norway breed, to rival the creature it so much resembles. Like that creature, it builds itself a cabin, but of a less perfect construction, and takes up its abode near the side of some piece of water. In the spring they leave their retreats, and in pairs subsist on leaves and roots till the summer comes on, when they feed on strawberries, rasberries, and such other fruits as they can reach. At the approach of winter they separate, when each takes up its lodging apart by itself in some hollow of a tree, where they remain quite unprovided with food, and there is the greatest reason to believe, subsist without any till the return of spring.

SQUIRRELS. There are five sorts of squirrels in America; the red, the grey, the black, the variegated, and the flying. The two former are exactly the same as those of Europe; the black are somewhat larger, and differ from them only in colour; the variegated also resemble them in shape and figure, but are very beautiful, being finely striped with white or grey, and sometimes with red and black. The American flying squirrel is much less than the European, being not above five inches long, and of a russet grey or ash-colour on the back, and white on the under parts. By a membrane on each side which reaches from its fore to its hind legs, this creature is enabled to leap from one tree to another, even if they stand a considerable distance apart.

The BEAVER. The beaver is an amphibious quadruped which cannot live for any long time in the water, and it is said is even able to exist entirely without it, provided it has the convenience of sometimes bathing itself. The largest beavers are nearly four feet in length, and about fourteen or fifteen inches in breadth over the haunches; they weigh about sixty pounds. Its head is like that of the otter, but larger; its snout is pretty long, the eyes small, the ears short, round, hairy on the outside, and smooth within, and its teeth very long; the under teeth stand out of their mouths about the breadth of three fingers, and the upper half a finger, all of which are broad, crooked, strong, and sharp; besides those teeth called the incisors, which grow double, are set very deep in their jaws, and bend like the edge of an axe, they have sixteen grinders, eight on each side, four above and four below, directly opposite to each other. With the former they are able to cut down trees of a considerable size, with the latter to break the hardest substances.

The ingenuity of these creatures in building their cabins, and in providing for their subsistence, is truly wonderful. When they are about to chuse themselves a habitation, they assemble in companies sometimes of two or three hundred and, after mature deliberation, fix on a place where plenty of provisions and all necessaries are to be found. Their houses are always situated in the water and when they can find neither lake nor pond adjacent, they endeavour to supply the defect by stopping the current of some brook or small river by means of a causeway or dam. For this purpose they set about felling of trees, and they take care to chuse out those that grow above the place where they intend to build, that they might swim down with the current. Having fixed on those that are proper, three or four beavers, placing themselves round a large one, find means with their strong teeth to bring it down. After they have by a continuance of the same labour and industry cut it into proper lengths, they roll these into the water and navigate them towards the place where they are to be employed.

The formation of their cabins is no less amazing. The figure of them is round or oval. Two thirds of the edifice stands above the water and this part is sufficiently capacious to contain eight or ten inhabitants. Each beaver has his place assigned him, the floor of which he curiously strews with leaves or small branches of the pine tree so as to render it clean and comfortable. Was I to enumerate every instance of sagacity that is to be discovered in these animals, they would fill a volume and prove not only entertaining but instructive.

The OTTER. This creature also is amphibious and greatly resembles a beaver, but is very different from it in many respects. The muzzle, eyes, and the form of the head are nearly the same but the teeth are very unlike, for the otter wants the large incisors or nippers that a beaver has. Instead of these, all his teeth, without any distinction, are shaped like those of a dog or wolf. The hair also of the former is not half so long as that belonging to the latter, nor is the colour exactly the same, for the hair of the otter under the neck, stomach, and belly is more greyish. This animal, which is met with in most parts of the world, but in much greater numbers in North America, is very mischievous and, when he is closely pursued, will not only attack dogs but men. Its flesh both tastes and smells of fish and is not wholsome food, though it is sometimes eaten through necessity.

The MINK is of the otter kind. In shape and size it resembles a pole-cat, being equally long and slender. Its skin is blacker than that of an otter, or almost any other creature, "as black as a mink" being a proverbial expression in America. It is not however so valuable. An agreeable musky scent exhales from its body and it is met with near the sources of rivers on whose banks it chiefly lives.

The Probability of the Interior Parts of North America Becoming Commercial Colonies and the Means by Which This Might Be Effected

THE COUNTRIES that lie between the great lakes and River Mississippi, and from thence southward to West Florida, although in the midst of a large continent and at a great distance from the sea, are so situated, that a communication between them and other realms might conveniently be opened, by which means those empires or colonies that may hereafter be founded or planted therein, will be rendered commercial ones. The great River Mississippi, which runs through the whole of them, will enable their inhabitants to establish an intercourse with foreign climes, equally as well as the Euphrates, the Nile, the Danube, or the Wolga do those people which dwell on their banks and who have no other convenience for exporting the produce of their own country or for importing those of others than boats and vessels of light burden, notwithstanding which they have become powerful and opulent states.

The Mississippi, as I have before observed, runs from north to south, and passes through the most fertile and temperate part of North America, excluding only the extremities of it, which verge both on the torrid and frigid zones. Thus favourably situated, when once its banks are covered with inhabitants, they need not long be at a loss for means to establish an extensive and profitable commerce. They will find the country towards the south almost spontaneously producing silk, cotton, indico, and tobacco; and the more northern parts, wine, oil, beef, tallow, skins, buffalo-wool, and furs; with lead, copper, iron, coals, lumber, corn, rice, and fruits, besides earth and barks for dying.

These articles, with which it abounds even to profusion, may be transported to the ocean through this river without greater difficulty than that which attends the conveyance of merchandize down some of those I have just mentioned. It is true that the Mississippi being the boundary between the English and Spanish settlements, and the Spaniards in possession of the mouth of it, they may obstruct the passage of it, and greatly dishearten those who make the first attempts. Yet when the advantages that will certainly arise to settlers are known, multitudes of adventurers, allured by the prospect of such abundant riches, will flock to it and establish themselves, though at the expence of rivers of blood.

But should the nation that happens to be in possession of New Orleans prove unfriendly to the internal settlers, they may find a way into the Gulph of Mexico after passing through Lake Maurepas into Lake Ponchartrain which has a communication with the sea within the borders of West Florida.

Although the English have acquired since the last peace a more extensive knowledge of the interior parts than were ever obtained before, even by the French, yet many of their productions still remain unknown. And though I was not deficient either in assiduity or attention during the short time I remained in them, yet I must acknowledge that the intelligence I gained was not so perfect as I could wish, and that it requires further researches to make the world thoroughly acquainted with the real value of these long hidden realms.

After the description of this delightful country I have already given, I need not repeat that all the spots I have thus pointed out as proper for colonization abound not only with the necessities of life, being well stored with rice, deer, buffalos, bears, &c. but produce in equal abundance such as may be termed luxuries, or at least those articles of commerce before recited which the inhabitants of it will have an opportunity of exchanging for the needful productions of other countries.

The discovery of a north-west passage to India has been the subject of innumerable disquisitions. Many efforts likewise have been made by way of Hudson's Bay to penetrate into the Pacific Ocean without success. I shall not therefore trouble myself to enumerate the advantages that would result from this much wished-for discovery, its utility being already too well known to the commercial world to need any elucidation. I shall only confine myself to the methods that appear most probable to ensure success to future adventurers.

The many attempts that have hitherto been made for this purpose, but which have all been rendered abortive, seem to have turned the spirit of making useful researches into another channel and this most interesting one has almost been given up as impracticable. But in my opinion, their failure rather proceeds from their being begun at an improper place than from their impracticability.

All navigators that have hitherto gone in search of this passage, have first entered Hudson's Bay, the consequence of which has been that without discovering any opening, terrified at the approach of winter, they have hastened back for fear of being frozen up. These apprehensions have discouraged the boldest adventurers from completing the expeditions in which they have engaged and frustrated every attempt. But as it has been discovered by such as have sailed into the northern parts of the Pacific Ocean that there are many inlets which verge towards Hudson's Bay, it is not to be doubted but that a passage might be made out from that quarter, if it be sought for at a proper season. And should these expectations be disappointed, the explorers would not be in the same hazardous situation with those who set out from Hudson's Bay, for they will always be sure of a safe retreat through an open sea to warmer regions, even after repeated disappointments. And this confidence will enable them to proceed with greater resolution, and probably be the means of effecting what too much circumspection or timidity has prevented.

BIBLIOGRAPHY

Browning, William. "The Early History of Jonathan Carver." *Wisconsin Magazine of History*. March, 1920.

Burpee, Lawrence. *The Search for the Western Sea*. Toronto, 1935.

Carver, Jonathan. *Travels Through the Interior Parts of North America*. London, 1781. (Also other editions.)

————. Manuscript Journals. Additional Manuscripts 8949 and 8950, Manuscript Students' Room, British Museum, London.

Cuneo, John R. *Robert Rogers of the Rangers*. New York, 1959.

Folwell, William Watts. *History of Minnesota*. St. Paul, 1921.

Greely, A. W. *Explorers and Travellers*. New York, 1893.

Hawke, David. *The Colonial Experience*. New York, 1966.

Hodge, F. W., ed. *Handbook of American Indians, North of Mexico*. Totowa, N.J., 1975.

Kellogg, Louise P. *The British Regime in Wisconsin*. Madison, 1935.

————. "The Mission of Jonathan Carver." *Wisconsin Magazine of History*. December, 1928.

Lee, John T. "A Bibliography of Carver's Travels." *Proceedings*. Madison, 1909.

————. "Captain Jonathan Carver: Additional Data." *Proceedings*. Madison, 1913.

Long, John. *Voyages and Travels of an Indian Intepreter and Trader*. London, 1791.

Parker, John, ed. *The Journals of Jonathan Carver and Related Documents*. St. Paul, 1976.

Public Record Office, London. Items CO 391-76:130, CO 391-77:19, and T1-475:240, concerning Carver's petitions to the British government.

Quaife, Milo M. "Jonathan Carver and the Carver Grant." *Mississippi Valley Historical Review*. June, 1920.

Sheldon, George. *History of Deerfield, Massachusetts*. Vol. 2. Deerfield, 1896.

Ver Steeg, Clarence L. *The Formative Years*. New York, 1964.

Williams, Glynwr. *The British Search for the Northwest Passage in the Eighteenth Century*. London, 1962.

INDEX

journal of travels, 23–24, 29, 36,
42–46. *See also Travels Through
the Interior Parts of North America*
lasting significance of, 50–51
letter to first wife, 26–27, 33, 47
in London, 33, 35, 36–38, 39,
107–8
maps and charts by, 17, 19, 20, 36,
57–58
in Massachusetts militia, 6, 13
mediation between Indian tribes,
47–48, 80–82, 92
recognition of, 44
reimbursement petitions to Crown,
33, 36–38, 41, 61, 64–65
return to Boston (1768), 107
return to Michilimackinac (1767),
26, 104–5
and Rogers' arrest, 28–29, 32
Rogers' specific commission to, 20–
21, 24, 25–26, 36–37, 60, 64
speech to Naudowessies, 90–92
stay with Naudowessies, 23–24, 25,
26–27, 87, 88–93
as visionary, 50
wife and children (British), 41, 44,
45
wife and heirs (American), 12, 26–
27, 28, 33, 40, 41, 49, 50
as writer of first popular American
travel book, 46
writings by, 44. *See also* subhead
journal of travels above
Carver, Mary Harris (second wife),
41, 44, 45, 47, 49
Carver, Robert, 12
Carver, Rufus (son), 40
Casse Tete. *See* war-club
Catholicism, 4
cat of the mountain, described, 217
cave (Dwelling of the Great Spirit),
82, 89
Charlevoix, Pierre de, 47
Chatham, Earl of, 42

Cherokee Indians, 174
cherries de sable. *See* sand cherries
chichicoue ceremony, 193, 200
Chickasaw Indians, 174
chief, 132–33
Carver as honorary Naudowessie
(Sioux), 23, 90, 189
Chipeway (Chippewa), 94, 104
dance tribute to, 142–43
feasts, 137
hunting preparations, 146
Killistino (Kilistinon), 103
name adoption, 189
Naudowessie (Sioux) system, 23
Naudowessie (Sioux) tent, 119
oration for dead colleague, 204
oration when facing death, 203
in peace process, 171, 175, 176
polygamy, 183–84
treatment of slave prisoners, 169
warfare role, 152, 154, 156
wedding ceremony role, 186
woman as, 21, 70, 73, 133
childbirth, 121, 200–201
children
carrying mother's name, 188, 189
custody practices, 185, 187
devotion to, 188–89, 210
newborn's cradles, 121–22
parental mourning, 206–7
treatment as prisoners, 168
Chipeway (Chippewa) Indians
Carver's contacts with, 25, 26, 94
character and temperament, 209–12
dancing style, 138
dispute with Naudowessies, 47–48,
80–82, 92
hieroglyphic messages, 213–14
language, 63, 70
and Michilimackinac, 63, 64, 94
peace mediation, 171–74
Supreme Being, 192
territory, 68, 93, 104
town description, 96

prisoner-taking, Indian practices,
160, 161–70
final disposition of living, 167–68
songs of, 163, 164, 165–66
tormenting/killing, 164–66
treatment of English women, 167
worth as barter, 169–70
Proclamation Line, 11
property rights
Indian equity views, 127–28
and war motivation, 153
pumpkins, 71

Queen's American Rangers (Rogers'
unit), 40–41

raccoon, 136
described, 220
rain of ink, 106
Randolph, John, 41
rattlesnakes, 73–74, 106
red fox, 216
Red Mountain, 95–96
red stone, 95, 96
red wood. See willow
religion, Indian, 191–95
afterlife concept, 192–93, 205,
206
anecdotes about, 73–74, 75
good and bad spirits, 27, 89, 192,
194, 200
Killistino priest's contact with Great
Spirit, 100–102
peace council role, 175–76
and warfare, 155, 156, 158
Winnebago prince's offerings, 83–
84
revenge, 133, 170, 175
as war motive, 153–54, 210, 211
rice. See wild rice
River Bands. See Naudowessie (Sioux)
Indians
River of the West. See Oregon
(Ourigan) River

rivers. See specific names by key
word, e.g. Mississippi River
Robbins, Abigail. See Carver, Abigail
Robbins
Roberts, Benjamin, 27, 28
Rogers, Elizabeth, 20
Rogers, Robert
arrest and acquittal, 28–29, 32, 33
background, 14
commission to Carver, 20–21, 24,
25–26, 36–37, 60, 64
dealings with Indians, 25
death in London, 41
enemies of, 27–28
financial debts and problems, 15,
40
Johnson and, 27
as Michilimackinac commandant,
17, 20, 27–28
Northwest Passage search plan, 13,
15–17, 18–19, 20, 21, 26, 43
return to America, 40–41
second Northwest Passage search
plan, 38–39, 40
Rogers' Rangers, 14–15
Ruggles, Timothy, 37
ruses and stratagems, Indian, 64, 71,
159–60, 161, 166, 172–73

Sacrifice Dance, 138
St. Anthony Falls. See Falls of St.
Anthony
St. Croix River, 25, 80, 96, 97
St. Francis River, 22, 87
St. Joseph island, 172
St. Joseph River, 20
St. Lawrence River, 60
St. Louis, 3
St. Marie Falls. See Falls of St.
Marie
St. Marie Straits, 104, 105, 172
St. Pierre River. See Minnesota River
salt, 135
sand cherries, 68